100
SCARIEST
THINGS ON
THE PLANET

Conceived, edited, and designed by Marshall Editions
The Old Brewery
6 Blundell Street
London N7 9BH

ISBN 978-0-545-37444-6

Publisher: James Ashton-Tyler
Editorial director: Sorrel Wood
Designers: Tim Scrivens, Ali Scrivens
Editorial project manager: Emily Collins
Production: Nikki Ingram

Printed and bound in China by Toppan Leefung Printers Ltd.

10 9 8 7 6 5 4 3 2 1   11 12 13 14 15

First edition, September 2011

Anna Claybourne

100 SCARIEST THINGS ON THE PLANET

CONTENTS

INTRODUCTION

What is scariness? There are lots of different ways of feeling scared. Suddenly spotting a spider could make you jump out of your skin. Being high up could make you feel dizzy. It all depends on who you are, and which things you find most frightening.

FEAR FACTOR

Fear is a strange feeling—it can be horrible, sickening, or gut churning, yet it can also be exciting, even fun! People often enjoy scaring themselves, whether it's by taking a daredevil roller coaster ride or watching a nail-biting thriller at the movies. This could be because these experiences let us face our fears and come out unharmed.

"FIGHT OR FLIGHT"

We have the ability to feel fear because it's useful—it makes us ready to deal with dangerous or scary things. This is sometimes called the "fight or flight" response. When you're scared, your heart beats faster, you breathe faster, and you may start to sweat.

THE FUNCTION OF FEAR

These things are actually preparing your body to run fast if you need to get away quickly, or to take on an enemy if you are attacked. Your fast breathing and heart rate send more oxygen to your cells, so your muscles can get you moving. Slightly sweaty hands will help you grip if you're in a struggle or trying to climb to safety.

WARNING!

Some of the things you'll read about in this book are scary for a very good reason—they really are dangerous! People who do extreme sports and risky stunts have a lot of training and important safety equipment. These are NOT things you should try! Don't attempt to copy anything dangerous that you see in this book.

Two BASE jumpers fearlessly launch themselves from Jin Mao Tower in Shanghai, China.

A PHOBIA?

A phobia is an intense, extreme fear that is out of proportion to the risk involved. Phobias of things like heights, spiders, mice, bridges, or elevators are quite common. Even if the phobia sufferer is completely safe, the thing they fear turns their legs to jelly, and they may panic, cry, or curl up in a ball. Some people have phobias of really strange things, like birds, beards, or even bananas! It might sound funny, but it can be horrible living with a phobia, as you never know when you might come across the thing that terrifies you.

SCARINESS RATING

😨 .A little bit scary!

😨😨 . . . . Really frightening!

😨😨😨 . . . . Seriously spine-tingling!

😨😨😨😨 . . . . . . .Horribly hair-raising!

😨😨😨😨😨 . . . . . .Totally terrifying!

SCARY NATURE AND FURIOUS FORCES

Being exposed to the raw power of nature can be downright terrifying—from feeling the world shake beneath you, to seeing the earth's insides bubble out of the ground. And the planet's creatures are just as fearsome. Imagine being chased by a swarm of deadly stinging bees!

ANTS

You might think ants can't really hurt you, and that tales of them swarming through towns and all over people are just from horror films. But it can really happen!

ARMY OF ANTS

The ants that do this are called army ants (or driver or safari ants). The scariest ones, found in Africa, live in huge groups that can contain an amazing 22 million ants. When they can't find enough food, they go on the march, moving in a huge "column," or line, through jungles, grasslands, and villages—or anything that's in their way.

DON'T BE ANT FOOD!

As they swarm, the ants surround other creatures and tear them up to eat. They mostly eat small animals, like other insects or spiders. But they will crawl all over anything in their path, and they can be dangerous. They cover about 66 feet (20 m) every hour. Most larger animals get out of the way fast, and so do any humans who see them coming.

Army ants can sting, but more importantly, you should watch out for their giant gnashers!

BRIDGING GAPS

Ants on the march can get across gaps or ponds by using their own bodies to form a living bridge.

SHARKS

This sand tiger shark has the sharpest, scariest-looking teeth ever!

When you're swimming in the sea, it's terrifying to think a giant killer shark might be swimming toward you! But would a shark really eat you?

SCARINESS

😨 😨 😨

Sharks have a scary reputation—bu most of them are not as dangerous as people think!

WHAT A LOT OF TEETH!

We think of sharks as fierce man-eaters mainly because of scary films—and because big sharks look so frightening, with their rows of razor-sharp teeth. And sharks do attack people sometimes. Around the world, there are about 60 shark attacks per year, and around 10 deaths.

SHARK SNACKS

The truth is, though, sharks don't like the taste of humans and usually avoid us. Most will only attack if they are confused and think you're a delicious animal, like a turtle or seal, or if they're very hungry. When they do attack, they usually only take one bite, then leave.

DID YOU KNOW? There are over 400 species (types) of sharks, but only a few, such as the great white shark, tiger shark, great hammerhead shark, and bull shark, are big and fierce enough to eat people. Some of the biggest sharks, like the whale shark, eat only tiny sea creatures.

SPIDERS

Some people are SO scared of spiders that they can't stand to be in a room with one. This fear is called arachnophobia, and it's one of the most common of all phobias (extreme fears).

ARE SPIDERS SAFE?

All spiders are hunters that feed on other animals, and they all have biting fangs. However, most spiders are very small, and harmless to humans. There are just a few, such as the Brazilian wandering spider, black widow, and Sydney funnel-web spider, that have a venomous bite strong enough to kill a person. Even then, most bites can be treated in the hospital, and you're very likely to survive.

SCARINESS

Creepy, crawly, fanged beasts that live all around us.

WHAT A FEAST!

Some people think spiders make a lovely snack! In parts of Cambodia, for example, they cook and eat them. Mmmm!

WHY ARE WE SCARED?

Some scientists believe we have learned over generations that some spiders can be dangerous, and this gives us an instinctive fear of all of them. But if you ask someone why they are scared of spiders, they usually just scream, "I can't stand all their wriggly legs and how fast they can run!"

Tarantulas can only swallow liquid food. They use their strong jaws to kill prey before sucking it up.

RATS

Rats are actually quite cute, so why are we horrified by them? It's mainly because wild rats are vermin—pests that hang around human homes and spread diseases.

REVOLTING RATS

It's not surprising that we find rats slightly gross. They nibble on garbage and live in stinky sewers full of toilet waste. They sneak into kitchens to steal food, and leave their disgusting droppings behind! They can be fairly big—up to 24 inches (60 cm) long including the tail—and they bite.

BRAINY BEASTS

Despite all this, rats are actually very clever animals. They're able to survive on our leftovers, and they will eat almost anything. They live in groups, play, cuddle for warmth, fight, and make noises to "talk." So in a lot of ways, they're a lot like us!

A big, fat brown rat, the most common species, and one of the largest.

SCARINESS

Finding a rat can give you a nasty scare!

FRIEND OF FOE? Most people find rats a little scary, but some people are completely terrified of them. A phobia of rats (or mice) is called musophobia. That said, some people love rats, and keep them as pets!

SNAKES

A snake's slender, slithery body, forked tongue, and hissing or rattling sound can make your palms sweat and the hairs stand up on the back of your neck. Snakes can suddenly dart forward to strike with their fangs. And plenty of them have a deadly bite.

USEFUL FEAR

Scientists have found that humans, even children and babies, are very good at spotting snakes in a series of pictures. They think humans may have developed this ability over time so that we now are born with it. In some parts of the world, venomous snakes are common, and being able to see and avoid them is very useful.

This European grass snake fakes death to lure in its prey!

CAUGHT BY A SNAKE!

Most snakes only bite when handled or threatened—or if you accidentally step on them. But there is a deadly snake, the bushmaster, from South and Central America, that can wait in hiding for weeks to ambush prey!

SCARINESS

Ssssnakes are scaly and slithery . . . and scary!

KEEP AWAY! If you see a snake, keep at least the snake's own body length away from it. Move away quickly, because they can strike fast!

BEES AND WASPS

Picnics are great, but there's one thing that can really ruin your fun. A bee or wasp buzzing around your food and your face, and making you flap frantically to scare it away! If you're scared of being stung, try not to worry—just one sting is not THAT bad.

WHY DO THEY STING?

Bees and wasps live in big family groups, called colonies. They help and defend one another, and will sting to protect the rest of their group. A honeybee dies after stinging a human, because its stinger gets stuck, which pulls the bee apart when it flies away. So it stings only if it really has to. Other bees and wasps can use their stingers many times—so beware.

THE WORST STINGS

A normal bee or wasp sting will hurt, and may make your skin swell up a little, but this won't last long. The tarantula hawk wasp and Asian giant hornet are much scarier! They're the world's biggest wasps, and can be up to 2 inches (5 cm) long! The hawk wasp's sting is said to be one of the most painful insect stings in the world, while the giant hornet's sting is one of the most venomous.

A vicious swarm of honeybees terrorizes an unfortunate victim.

SCARINESS

😨 😨

Don't panic, and they will buzz off!

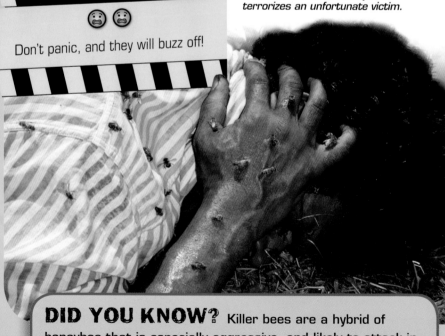

DID YOU KNOW? Killer bees are a hybrid of honeybee that is especially aggressive, and likely to attack in a swarm—if they all sting you at once, it can be deadly.

VOLCANOLOGY

Volcanologists (volcano scientists) sometimes work in a lab or office—but they also go out and study their subject in the real world. That means exploring active volcanoes, where they may have to dodge red-hot flowing lava.

LET'S GET OUT OF HERE! Luckily, volcanologists know a lot about volcanoes. They can often tell when they will erupt, and how risky they are. Some, such as Kilauea in Hawaii, erupt gently, and it's easy to avoid the lava. Others, like Etna in Italy, can erupt violently, sometimes showering volcanologists with rock fragments. Ouch! A few, such as Unzen in Japan, can take you by surprise. A sudden eruption there killed 3 volcanologists, along with 40 other people, in 1991.

SCARY VOLCANOES It's

not just eruptions that make volcanoes scary. They can get you in other ways, too!

• *Mudflows* Volcanic ash can mix with water to make fast-flowing mud floods.

• *Tsunamis* Landslides forced into the sea by a volcano can trigger a tsunami.

SCARINESS

Volcanologists mostly enjoy their work, although it can be deadly.

A volcanologist risking a roasting while collecting a lava sample.

VOLCANIC ERUPTION

We humans like to think we are in charge on our planet—but when you see a volcano erupt, you remember that there are some things we can't control! A volcanic eruption is one of nature's most violent and terrifying spectacles.

SCARINESS

Volcanoes just have so much scary stuff to throw at you!

LIQUID LAVA

In an eruption, pressure builds up inside until the volcano erupts (bursts), pouring out lava—rock that is melted into runny, glowing goop by the high temperatures inside the earth. Lava ranges from about 1,300 degrees Fahrenheit (700 degrees Celsius) to 2,200 degrees Fahrenheit (1,200 degrees Celsius)—five times hotter than the hottest kitchen oven. It can set fire to plants as it flows past them, or boil water when it hits rivers or the sea. So don't get too close! If you fell into lava, you would burn to a crisp.

ASHES, GASES, BLOCKS, AND BOMBS

As a volcano explodes, it flings out "blocks" of solid rock, as well as "bombs"—big blobs of lava that cool and harden as they fly through the air. It also releases burning hot gases and choking ash. Sometimes all of these combine in a fast-flowing "river," called a pyroclastic flow—one of the scariest types of volcanic eruption.

The erupting crater of Mount Etna, an active volcano in Sicily.

EARTHQUAKE

The ground seems solid and secure—certainly compared to some of the scary situations in this book! But even the ground doesn't always stay still. It can tremble, shudder, and shake, or even tear itself apart.

QUAKING AND SHAKING!

It can be really scary when you suddenly feel the ground shuddering and moving. In a small quake, things might fall off shelves, or a few windows might break. Really big earthquakes are much more serious, and can cause major destruction. Buildings crumble, bridges collapse, and cracks open up in the ground. Earthquakes can also cause other horrors, like landslides, floods, and tsunamis (see page 18).

PIE-CRUST EARTH

It's scary to think that the ground we walk around on can move. Earth's crust, or covering, is made up of huge sections of solid rock that float on top of the running rock inside Earth (like lava, but called magma). An earthquake happens when these sections collide, grind together, then suddenly slip. Hold on tight!

The scary destruction caused by an earthquake in California.

SCARINESS

...might just shake your house—or it could make the ground tear apart!

ANIMAL ALARMS

Dogs, cats, and other animals sometimes seem to be able to sense when an earthquake is about to happen. They become restless and nervous, or run away.

TSUNAMI

A tsunami happens when seawater is moved suddenly by something like an earthquake or volcanic eruption. Ripples spread out in a circle, until they become giant waves that crash onto the coast.

ROLLING RIPPLES

The strange thing about tsunamis is that when they're rolling across the ocean, they don't look like much. The ripple travels fast, but it's wide and low, rather than big and towering. If you were in a boat, it could go past and you might not even notice. The danger comes at the coast, where the water is shallower. The wave slows down, and the water it's carrying starts to gather together and pile up.

HOW HIGH?

Tsunami waves are usually up to 33 feet (10 m) high when they hit land, though they can be higher. Even a small one can be pretty scary, as it can flood the land, smashing houses and sweeping people—even cars—away.

A frighteningly giant wave heads toward land.

TSUNAMI ALERT!

Scientists are building better early warning systems that track tsunamis across the oceans and predict where and when they'll strike.

SCARINESS

😨 😨 😨 😨 😨

This giant wall of water is a terrifying killer.

The destruction caused by a tsunami in Hilo, Hawaii.

ROGUE WAVE

For centuries, sailors have told tales of giant waves that seemed to come from nowhere, drowning ships and sending seamen to a watery grave. Most people didn't believe them, and thought these rogue or "freak" waves were no more real than giant sea serpents. Now, though, we know that rogue waves do exist.

WHAT ARE THEY?

A rogue wave is a big wave—sometimes up to 100 feet (30 m) high, as tall as a 12-story building. But that's not why it's called "rogue." The reason these waves are so weird is that they happen out of the blue. They're much higher than other waves around them, and can go in a different direction and catch you off guard.

A ship battles against a rogue wave in the film The Perfect Storm.

BRAVING THE WAVE!

Because rogue waves are very hard to predict, people at sea don't know one is coming until it's almost on top of them—and it's a deadly, frightening experience. First the boat may slip down into a deep trough in front of the wave, making the wave tower even higher in relation. Then the boat can ride up the wave and overturn, or crash through it, sometimes getting smashed into pieces.

FREAK SPOTS?

Scientists aren't sure what causes rogue waves. They are more common in certain spots than in others.

SCARINESS

They come from nowhere— without warning!

FLASH FLOOD

A flash flood strikes suddenly, and can crash down on you out of the blue—even when it's not raining!

SUMMER SHOCK

Flash floods usually happen in hot weather, after thunderstorms and heavy rain. If a lot of rain falls quickly, especially somewhere hilly, streams and rivers that were almost empty can suddenly fill up. They flow downhill and gather together, forming a rushing mass of water. The flood can sweep away cars and houses.

WHAT HAPPENS

Imagine you're swimming in a shallow river on your vacation—or even just walking down a street in town. Suddenly, you hear a roaring sound behind you. You turn around and see a frothing, churning mass of water, taller than you are, heading toward you faster than you can run. Oh no!

SCARINESS

A flash flood strikes on dry land and leaves you little time to escape.

A flash flood descends on a busy street in Toowomba, near Brisbane, Australia, in January 2011.

KEEP LEFT

EXTRA VOLUME

Even scarier flash floods can happen if a dam collapses, releasing a vast amount of water all at once—or if an erupting volcano melts a lot of snow.

AVALANCHE

Maybe you think of snow as lovely, soft, fluffy stuff that's fun for sledding, snowballs, and making snowmen. Well, it can be! But if an avalanche of falling snow hits you, it's no fun at all. It's really dangerous, and, if you survive it, you could face the terror of being trapped underneath the snow.

AVALANCHE ALERT!

When snow falls on mountains, it collects in large piles, or packs. A lot of snow in one place is very heavy. After a long time, the pack collapses under the weight of the snow from later snowfalls. It all tumbles down the mountain at up to 80 mph (130 km/h).

STUCK IN THE SNOW

Avalanches can quickly crush and bury skiers, hikers, or snowboarders. If you do get buried, you might be lucky enough to have some space around you under the snow, so you can breathe—but you'll soon run out of air or begin to freeze.

SCARINESS

Snow looks pretty— but imagine all that falling on you!

An avalanche roars down K2 mountain in Pakistan.

ROOF AVALANCHE

Even in cities, you can get a scary amount of snow dumped on your head, from heavy snowfall on rooftops. If the snow gets too thick, or starts to thaw, it can suddenly slide off all at once.

METEORITE

A meteorite is an object that falls from space and crashes into the ground. It could be a speck of dust, a small rock (called a meteoroid when it's still in space), or a huge asteroid. Once it's hit the ground, it is known as a meteorite.

BURNING UP!

There are pieces of rock sailing through space all the time, and many get sucked in by Earth's gravity. However, most never land. As they fall through Earth's atmosphere, air friction heats them up until they burn to nothing in a blaze of light. *Phew!* You can sometimes see them at night, falling as shooting stars.

CLEAR THE RUNWAY

Some bigger rocks do make it down to the ground, zooming in at up to 30,000 mph (50,000 km/h), and become meteorites. That's a little scary, because one could fall on your house! But they are rare, and most of Earth's surface is ocean or empty land, so they rarely hit people. Much more scary is the risk of a really big space rock, called an asteroid, hitting our planet. That could blast whole cities, cause giant tsunamis (see page 18), or throw up dust clouds that would darken the sky and stop plants from growing for months.

SCARINESS

A meteorite could squash you flat! But don't worry too much— they're very rare.

A meteoroid zooming toward the ground could look just like this!

BOINK! Some lucky people have survived a meteorite strike. Recent examples include a 14-year-old boy whose hand was hit by a meteorite in Germany in 2009 and a 51-year-old man who was hit in the chest after one bounced off the ground as he watched a cricket match in England in 2010.

WILDFIRE

Fire is one of the most useful things humans have, but it's also one of the scariest when it gets out of control. A house catching on fire is bad enough. A big wildfire is even more frightening. It can devour a vast area of countryside or even set whole cities ablaze.

WHAT CAUSES THEM?

Wildfires (also called bushfires or forest fires) happen when grass, shrubs, or forests catch fire, usually after long periods of hot, dry weather. That's why they happen most often in places like California, Australia, and Greece. The spark that starts the fire burning can come from a lightning bolt or a volcanic eruption. But most wildfires start by themselves when dry grass or wood heats up. If wind fans the flames, the fire spreads fast.

STAY OR GO?

When wildfires spread close to people's homes, they're extremely frightening, and often claim lives. Sometimes people stay in their houses, spraying water on them to stop them from catching fire—but this doesn't always work.

SCARINESS

Being surrounded by a wildfire must be totally terrifying.

A wildfire rages in Victoria, Australia.

DON'T LITTER! The curved part of a glass bottle can act as a lens and focus the sun's heat in one spot, starting a fire. Sparks from campfires have also caused terrible fires.

BLIZZARD

Snow falling gently and quietly is a beautiful sight—especially when it's the first snow of the winter and you can't wait to get outside! A blizzard is different. It's a fierce snowstorm, with heavy snow and howling winds that blow it in every direction.

WHERE AM I?

One of the scariest things about a blizzard is that the air fills up so quickly with flying snow, you can't see where you're going. If there's deep snow on the ground as well, it's easy to get lost. Sometimes people very close to safety have lost their way in a blizzard because they had no idea where they were.

IN THE WILD

Blizzards are worse on high, snowy mountains and in Antarctica, the continent around the South Pole. They trap explorers for days.

SNOW JOKE

Captain Robert Scott and his team died in the Antarctic in 1912, after trekking to the South Pole. They were close to a food store that could have saved them, but a blizzard stopped them from going any farther. Scott wrote in his diary: "One cannot see the next tent, let alone the land. What on earth does such weather mean?"

SCARINESS

In a blizzard you can end up freezing, lost, and unable to see anything!

A jeep battles against a powerful blizzard in Iceland.

ICE STORM

An ice storm is a strange kind of storm. It happens in freezing temperatures, when very cold rain falls. It freezes wherever it lands, covering everything with ice. Roads, roofs, and trees all get a thick, heavy, glittery coating of ice.

WHY BE SCARED?

Ice storms can be bad news. The ice is heavy, and if there's a lot of it, it can make trees, power lines, and roofs break. Icy roads are dangerous to drive or walk on. Electricity and phone lines get cut off, and people can get stuck in their homes.

LIVE ELECTRICITY

One of the scariest things you can see in an ice storm is an overhead electricity cable that has snapped and fallen down. It can twist and spin around with sparks shooting out of it. If you see one, don't go near it—and get away as fast as you can!

SCARINESS

Ice storms can look stunning, but they are definitely scary!

TOP TIP! Don't stand around under tree branches during an ice storm. A branch or a huge chunk of ice could *cr-r-r-ACK* and fall on you.

A fierce ice storm in Nebraska in 2006 snapped this power line.

THUNDERSTORM

Have you ever hidden under the sheets, covering your ears to block out the sound during a thunderstorm? It's pretty scary when the sky goes black, rumbles, and roars, and giant electric sparks crash down from the clouds.

ELECTRIC STORM

A thunderstorm happens when warm, damp air rises high in the sky, making a thundercloud. As the water droplets rise, they bump around, giving the cloud an electrical charge. Lightning is a huge spark that jumps between an electrically charged cloud and the ground.

THE SOUND OF LIGHTNING

Thunder and lightning are actually the same thing—lightning is the spark you see, and thunder is the sound it makes.

A lightning strike can be deadly.

SCARINESS

Many people are really scared of thunder and lightning.

TAKE THAT, MORTALS! Long ago, people thought thunderstorms happened because the gods were angry. They roared and threw thunderbolts at humans to punish them.

SAINT ELMO'S FIRE

Saint Elmo's fire is a mysterious bluish glow, like a large gas flame. It can appear during a thunderstorm, at the top of something high and pointed, such as a ship's mast. It's not surprising that sailors long ago were sure it was something supernatural! However, they weren't too scared, since they thought it was a good omen.

ELECTRICAL ELMO

Like lightning, Saint Elmo's fire is actually a type of electricity. During a storm, electrical charge collects in the ship's mast, or around other high points, until there is a big difference in charge between the object and the air around it. Then electricity leaves the object and flows into the air, making it glow.

Saint Elmo's fire strikes during a thunderstorm.

HERE TO SAVE US!

Saint Elmo's fire usually appears toward the end of a thunderstorm. So sailors thought it was a signal that their prayers had been answered, and the storm would end soon.

SCARINESS

😨 😨

Saint Elmo's fire is a little eerie!

WINGS OF FIRE You might see Saint Elmo's fire around the wing tips of a plane when you're in the air. It can mean that lightning is about to strike the aircraft. Don't worry—airplanes are normally strong enough to handle it.

BALL LIGHTNING

Ball lightning usually happens during a thunderstorm—but unlike normal lightning, it can appear indoors. It can even pass through solid objects, such as walls and doors! It's been spotted in buildings, boats, and aircraft, as well as outside. So what is it?

BALL OF FIRE

People who've seen ball lightning say it looks like a strange glowing ball hovering in midair, or sometimes floating along. It can be as small as a tennis ball or as big as a beach ball. There are some reports of balls more than 3 feet (1 m) across. Scientists think ball lightning is electrical, but no one is really sure how it forms.

HISS!

The ball usually floats around for a few moments, before going *HISS!* and fizzling out. In most sightings, no one has been hurt. But some people, who tried to touch the ball or push it away, received a nasty burn.

IS IT REAL? Some scientists have argued that ball lightning could be an illusion, caused by thunderstorms having a strange effect on our brains and making us see dots in front of our eyes that aren't really there. But it has been caught on camera a few times.

SCARINESS

☹ ☹ ☹

Ball lightning is very spooky and strange—and it can be harmful, too

This photograph captures a spooky spark of ball lightning.

WILL·O'·THE·WISP

"Will-o'-the-wisp," "jack-o'-lantern," "corpse candle," "spook light," or "elf-fire"—these names show that in the past, people thought this mysterious, glowing light was some kind of ghost, fairy, or magical creature. It looks like a faint, flickering flame that hovers above the ground in marshy or swampy areas.

GOOD OR BAD?

According to some old folktales, will-o'-the-wisps are mischievous, even evil, spirits that lure people into dangerous marshy land. They are said to move away when you get close to them so that you follow them farther, then disappear once you're stuck in the swamp! In tales from other countries, the lights were also known as "treasure fire," and were said to show where piles of treasure were buried.

WHAT IS IT REALLY?

No one is 100 percent sure what causes a will-o'-the-wisp, but most scientists think they are made of gas from rotting plants, bubbling out of swamps and marshes. It may somehow light up or catch fire, though many reports say will-o'-the-wisps are not hot. This theory also doesn't explain why they appear to move around. So they're still somewhat mysterious!

A will-o'-the-wisp glows bright in the marshes.

ANCIENT FIRES

Long ago, many people had seen a will-o'-the-wisp, which is why there are so many stories. Today, few people have because we live farther away from marshes.

SCARINESS

A spooky light in the night!

RAINING FISH

It might sound impossible, but it really is true that showers of fish can fall out of the sky. It's been reported many times through history, in lots of different countries. So-called fish falls aren't usually dangerous, but they're scary because they're so strange.

FISH TALES

Reports of fish falls date back thousands of years. The Roman writer Pliny the Elder and the Greek historian Athenaeus both described them almost 2,000 years ago. Fish fell in various parts of the United States in the 1800s, including squid that is said to have hit Pennsylvania in 1841. In 2000, a huge fish fall landed on farmland in Ethiopia, Africa.

SNAKES IN THE RAIN

Fish aren't the only kind of bizarre rainfall. Falls of frogs, lizards, snakes, and strange jellies have also been reported around the world.

SCARINESS

Raining fish could be horrible if a large fish whacks you on the head

WHAT'S GOING ON?

Amazingly, there is a scientific explanation! The fish are thought to be scooped up by waterspouts, which are powerful, tornadolike windstorms that form over water. A waterspout could suck water and fish from the sea or a river and carry them through the sky for some distance, until the fish fall like rain.

Fish cover the ground after a spooky shower.

BLOOD RAIN

When rain as red as blood falls from the sky, it's not surprising that people are a little alarmed. This has been happening for centuries. In the past, it was seen as a bad omen, a warning from the gods that something terrible was about to happen.

HOW RED IS IT?

Sometimes, blood rain really is bright red, like blood. It can also be a faint red or a brownish color. The most famous blood rain of recent times hit Kerala, part of India, in 2001. It fell for two months, staining plants and clothes pink!

EXPLAIN THE RAIN!

Why is the rain red? Some people think rainwater mixes with dust from a desert or dust that has showered down from an exploding meteoroid. But tests show the rain contains what looks like tiny red cells. Some experts believe they come from a type of reddish algae, a simple plantlike creature. But no one is sure how they get into the sky.

SCARINESS

No one wants to be caught in a shower of bloodred rain.

Blood rain as bright as this could certainly dye your clothes pink.

RAIN FROM OUTER SPACE

Some scientists believe the rain contains bacteria that must have been transported from space by a comet.

SOLAR ECLIPSE

It's the middle of a warm, sunny day. Then, suddenly, something very strange happens. It starts to get dark. It's not just a cloud— the sun is actually going out! Gradually, more and more of it disappears, until you can see the stars—but it's only lunchtime!

DARKNESS TO COME

It's no wonder that ancient people found this terrifying—they depended on the sun for light and warmth and to make their crops grow, just like we do. Luckily, though, an eclipse doesn't last long and the sun does reappear afterward. But, as with so many other strange natural events, many people believed an eclipse was a warning of doom.

HOW DOES IT WORK?

A solar eclipse happens when the moon passes in between Earth and the sun. The moon is exactly the right size to cover up the sun. (It's a lot smaller than the sun, of course, but it's also a lot nearer, making it look the same size.) The sun looks black and you can see only the corona, the ring of flames and gases around the edge.

SCARINESS

An eclipse is superscary if you don't know what's happening because it looks like the sun has disappeared

ANCIENT MATH

Even in ancient times, some astronomers figured out the real cause of a solar eclipse and learned to predict when the next one would happen.

RED SPRITES AND BLUE JETS

Red sprites and blue jets sound like something from a sci-fi movie—and they look that way, too! A red sprite is an enormous red flash high in the sky, shaped like a jellyfish, with a wide ring-shaped "body" and trailing "tentacles." A blue jet is a bright blue flash or spark that zooms upward. These strange sights have been spotted by telescopes at night, and by planes and spacecraft.

THE ALIENS ARE HERE!

These unearthly flashes could be mistaken for flying saucers or alien rockets, but they're not either of these things. They only appear for a very short time—sometimes less than a second—and are definitely made of light, not something solid.

WHAT CAUSES THEM?

Red sprites and blue jets appear above thunderstorms. They are caused by electrical energy and linked to lightning strikes. In fact, they are considered to be a type of lightning.

SCARINESS

A very peculiar phenomenon—but so high, we rarely see them.

A red sprite flashes in the sky.

TOP TIP! It's possible to see red sprites and blue jets from the ground, if you're in a place where you can see a really long way and have a good view of a faraway thunderstorm. Look high above the thunderstorm.

GIANT HAIL

Hail normally means a shower of pea-size balls of ice falling. If they hit you on the head, it can hurt. So imagine what it's like in a storm of giant hailstones bigger than golf balls!

HORROR HAIL

In 2010, a shower of hailstones up to 1.5 inches (4 cm) across fell on Perth, Australia, smashing windows, cars, and roofs. A storm of egg-size hail in China killed 25 people in 2002. Giant hail will also flatten crops.

SCARINESS

Being stuck in a storm of giant hailstones would be petrifying!

LAYERS OF ICE

Hailstones form in thunderclouds when cold water freezes around a tiny object such as a speck of dust. The hailstone then bounces around inside the cloud, building up more layers of ice, and getting bigger and bigger. Sometimes hailstones can grow to 2–4 inches (5–10 cm) across. The biggest hailstones of all, though, are made of lots of smaller hailstones that have clumped together.

The hood of this car has been pounded by giant hailstones.

DUCK AND COVER If you are ever caught out in a storm of giant hail, run indoors if you can, find an enclosed bus stop, or even crawl under a park bench if you have to.

SANDSTORM

Sandstorms start in dry, sandy places when there's a strong, long-lasting wind. As one starts, grains of sand are blown over the ground. As they roll, bump, and bounce along, they loosen more and more grains of sand. The smaller sand particles get carried into the air, while the bigger ones tumble along at a lower level.

ON THE MOVE

Once a sandstorm starts, you'll soon have a huge, moving mass of sand blowing across the land. It can be over a mile (1.6 km) tall and move at 60 mph (97 km/h). When you see a sandstorm this big approaching, it's terrifying. Get somewhere safe as fast as you can!

DUSTY VIEW

Sandstorms can clog the air, making it hard to breathe, or even dump enough sand to bury cars and homes. The flying sand makes it hard to see where you're going, causing car crashes. Airports have to be closed and crops can be destroyed.

SCARINESS

sandstorm rolling in can be a really scary sight.

A menacing sandstorm moves over the desert in Eritrea, Africa.

GLOBAL ISSUE Sandstorms are most common in China, northern Africa, and the Arabian Peninsula—but they also happen in the United States and anywhere with deserts.

SCARY PLACES AND DREADFUL DESTINATIONS

There's lots of scary exploring to be done in haunted castles and deep, dark caves. Imagine having to climb a rope bridge to get to school, or being able to stand above the Grand Canyon—and see all the way down!

CLIFFS OF MOHER

These amazing cliffs are on the west coast of Ireland, where it meets the Atlantic Ocean. They're huge! They rise to more than 680 feet (210 m) high, as tall as a skyscraper, and stretch for nearly 5 miles (8 km) along the coast. They're also unusually vertical, so in many places it's a sheer drop to the rocks below.

DON'T LOOK DOWN!

The Cliffs of Moher are a top tourist attraction in Ireland, and thousands of people visit them every year. There's a cliff walk along the top, with breathtaking views. However, some people ignore the safety warnings and take unofficial routes too close to the edge. This is very dangerous, as rocks can fall off the cliffs, and it can also be extremely windy.

Two tourists lie down to view the sheer drop below.

TOURIST TOWER

Visitors have flocked to see the cliffs for decades. A local landowner, Cornelius O'Brien, built a tower, O'Brien's Tower, to draw more tourists to the area. Climbing this tower gives you an even better view.

SCARINESS

Beautiful, breathtaking, but also bloodcurdlingly scary cliffs!

YUNGAS ROAD

Imagine you're driving along a cliffside road that is only 10 feet (3 m) wide, with no barriers at the edge. Even worse, it's made of crumbly mud, and the rocks at the edge are loose! One false move and you'll topple over the side—a 3,000-foot (900 m) drop into a dark ravine.

ROAD OF DEATH
This isn't a scene from a movie—it's a real place: Yungas Road in Bolivia, South America. The nearly 50-mile (80 km) road leads from the country's capital, La Paz, to Coroico in the Yungas district, winding along the sides of almost vertical cliffs. The locals call it "El Camino de la Muerte," or "the Road of Death," and it's renowned as the deadliest road in the world.

DRIVE SAFELY!
Although the road is obviously dangerous, many people still take hair-raising risks, passing other cars and zooming around corners. And every year, some cars and trucks do fall off. The road has claimed thousands of lives.

SCARINESS
😨 😨 😨 😨 😨

The worst place in the world to los control of the wheel!

ALTERNATIVE ROUTE In 2006, a new road was created to avoid the worst areas of the deadly Yungas Road, making it safer. But people still use the old road as a shortcut, and tourists go to drive or bike along it for thrills.

GUOLIANG TUNNEL

Until 1972, the only way to reach the tiny Chinese village of Guoliang was to climb the "sky ladder"—a set of stone steps cut into the cliff. The villagers spent five years hammering away at the rock, creating a tunnel road just over 0.5 mile (1 km) long.

SCARINESS

A pretty scary road, especially if you're not comfortable on a cliff edge.

LIGHT AND SHADE

The cliff-edge road is superscary in places—but also spooky and strangely beautiful. Spots of sunlight and shade dapple the track through windows carved in the rock. The road has a spectacular view down a gorge.

STONE WORLD

Because Guoliang village was isolated in the mountains for so long, people had to use stone to make most of their everyday items. As well as stone houses, they made stone furniture!

TOURIST TUNNEL

As well as linking the village to a main road so that supplies can get in, the road is now open to tourists. Thousands of people visit each year to experience the amazing road for themselves, and to see the ancient village.

Guoliang Tunnel Road weaving its way along the cliff.

TROLLSTIGEN ROAD

"Trollstigen" means "troll ladder," and this road, zigzagging up an incredibly steep mountainside in Norway, is a bit like a ladder. But it's a real road, with big trucks and buses driving around its hairpin bends and along its scary precipices. The views are amazing.

CLIMBING THE LADDER

The road is narrow in places, and large vehicles have to *squeeeeeze* past one another to get up and down. When you get to the top, there's a parking lot and scenic lookout where you can stand and watch near misses on the twists and turns of the road below.

WHAT HAVE TROLLS GOT TO DO WITH IT?

In Norwegian folktales, trolls are ugly, dwarflike creatures that live in the mountains. Norway has other features named after trolls, too, such as the Trollveggen cliff (Troll Wall) and Troll Valley. Trolls are scary, too! But luckily, they're not real.

The Trollstigen winds its way up the mountainside.

SCARINESS

Terrifying if you don't like heights, but otherwise not too bad.

ROAD AHEAD CLOSED! The Trollstigen Road is only open for about half the year. In winter it's so snowy and icy, it would be a disaster to drive on.

EL CAMINO DEL REY

To walk along the Camino del Rey in Spain, you truly need nerves of steel. It's a narrow, rickety pathway clinging to the side of a cliff, above a sheer 325-foot (100 m) drop. There's no handrail, and even scarier, parts of the path have collapsed!

SCARINESS

😨 😨 😨 😨 😨

One of the scariest walks anywhere in the world.

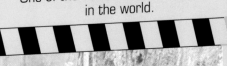

DEADLY DANGEROUS

The Camino, or Caminito (meaning "little pathway"), is so badly damaged, it's no longer used as a proper path. But lots of climbers and people who love extreme sports have headed there, hoping to walk all the way along its 2 miles (3 km) as a challenge or dare. There is a wire fixed to the cliff, which they can attach themselves to with a climbing rope, making the journey slightly safer. But still, quite a few people have fallen off.

Be careful! A foolhardy adventurer treads carefully along the path.

FIT FOR A KING The pathway was built in 1901–1905 to link two power plants in the mountains of southern Spain. It allowed workers to carry equipment to and fro. But it only got its famous name in 1921, when Spain's King Alfonso XIII walked along it. El Camino del Rey means "the king's path."

TRIFT BRIDGE

Switzerland's Trift Bridge is a famously high, long, and terrifying rope bridge across a mountain gorge in the Alps. Bridges like this can be found worldwide, and are just for pedestrians. There are two cables, or ropes, to hold on to, and a narrow walkway dangling in between. When you walk across, you can peer through the gaps, 330 feet (100 m) down to the rushing river and lake below.

TOP TIP! Walking along a narrow rope bridge can make it bounce and sway. If you don't like that much, try "gliding," or edging your feet forward, instead of walking normally.

BRIDGE 1: 2004

There have actually been two Trift bridges. The first one was too scary, so they made it longer and higher! How does that work? Well, the first, 230-foot (70 m) high bridge was built in 2004 so that walkers could reach a mountain hut nearby. Unfortunately, it crossed a narrow part of the gorge where winds rushed through at high speeds, making the bridge wobble. Meanwhile, thousands of tourists kept turning up to walk across the bridge. It needed to be stronger and safer . . .

Walkers hold on tight as they make the Trift Bridge crossing.

BRIDGE 2: 2009

. . . so in 2009 the bridge was replaced with a new one higher up, in a less windy part of the gorge. It has extra cables attached to it. It is now almost 560 feet (170 m) long.

SCARINESS

You need some courage to cross t bridge, but it's actually fairly saf

HUSSAINI BRIDGE

SCARINESS

is bridge is seriously frightening—
t just a normal route for the locals.

A local makes his way over the wobbly planks of the bridge.

Imagine if you had to get across THIS anytime you wanted to go shopping! It's the Hussaini Hanging Bridge in Pakistan, renowned as one of the scariest bridges in the world. No one is sure exactly how many people have fallen off it and plunged into the icy water below. The bridge is very old and gets lots of use.

FALLING TO PIECES

One reason this bridge is so scary is that it's not in great shape. The walkway is made of wobbly, uneven planks and logs, loosely strung together with ropes and wires. Some of the planks and ropes are missing and broken, and the bridge has been frequently repaired and patched up.

BRRRR!

To make matters worse, the bridge is in Pakistan's mountains, where it's very windy. The gusty wind can blow you off the bridge into the lake, which is so cold, you can't survive in it for long.

A BETTER BRIDGE? Soon, the Hussaini Bridge could be replaced with something stronger. So tourists who want to try it out might not have much time left!

TIANMEN SHAN CABLE CAR

When you get on this cable-car ride in the Chinese city of Zhangjiajie, it doesn't seem all that scary at first. The cabin sails over the city, then the surrounding farmland, where you can wave to workers in the fields. But then it starts to climb up among the mountains, toward the towering peak of Tianmen Shan—"Heaven's Gate Mountain."

HIGH IN THE SKY

Before long, you're dangling hundreds of feet up in the air, with nothing below you but jagged mountain rocks—and a few clouds. Eek! In fact, this cable car is one of the world's highest and longest—it's more than 4.5 miles (7 km) long and rises over 4,900 feet (1,500 m).

UP TO THE TOP

The cable car carries you almost to the top of the mountain, where there's an amazing cliff-top park with lots more hair-raising thrills, such as cliffside walkways and overhanging viewing platforms. There's also the Heaven's Gate itself, a stunning natural archway in the rock.

A breathtaking view from the cable car on a frosty morning.

SCARINESS

A mixture of gut-churningly scary and incredibly beautiful and exhilarating.

STAY PUT! If you are ever in a cable car that gets stuck, **STAY THERE!** You'll be rescued. Trying to get to safety yourself is a recipe for disaster.

NGONG PING 360

Hold on tight as you begin your ride on the Ngong Ping 360—a cable car that has a view 360 degrees all around. The Ngong Ping 360, in Hong Kong, is designed to give tourists an exciting ride, from Lantau Island up to the top of the 1,650-foot-high (500 m) Ngong Ping plateau.

NOT SCARED YET?

Then maybe you need a Crystal Cabin. These extra-special cable cars have a clear floor, so as well as seeing a 360-degree view through all the side windows, you can watch the world go by beneath your feet. There's a view of Tung Chung and the South China Sea, and you can look down on planes as they land at the airport.

OOPS!

In 2007, one of Ngong Ping's cable cars fell off its cable. It plummeted 165 feet (50 m)—the height of a 16-story apartment building—to the ground near the ride's terminal. CRASH! Luckily, it's not as bad as it sounds—there was no one inside. The system had been closed for the night an hour earlier, and engineers were carrying out tests. Since then, safety has been improved.

SCARINESS

😰 😰

A cool cable-car ride, but a little scary, too!

Ngong Ping 360 cabins sail through the sky.

ARE CABLE CARS SAFE? Yes—despite the scary Ngong Ping accident, they're actually very safe. Being high up in a dangly cable car might make your stomach flip, but in fact you're safe.

GRAND CANYON SKYWALK

If you go to the Grand Canyon Skywalk in Arizona, you can stand in midair, hundreds of feet above the floor of the vast Grand Canyon valley. The U-shaped walkway sticks out 70 feet (20 m) over the edge of a sheer cliff, and has a glass floor. Would you dare?

BUILT TO THRILL

The skywalk opened in 2007, and was built by the Hualapai Native American people. The walkway is made of six layers of superstrength glass, each tough enough to stop a bullet!

DOWN THROUGH THE GLASS

Why are glass floors so scary? When you look down and see nothing but a huge drop, your brain can't help thinking you're in danger. You start sweating and your heart beats faster—even if you know you're safe. After all, no one would build a tourist attraction like this without making sure it could take the weight of crowds of tourists.

There can be as many as 120 people on the skywalk at any one time.

SCARINESS

Your legs could turn to jelly just thinking about it!

Visitors must wear special slippers when walking on the glass.

CN TOWER

The CN Tower reaches high above the skyline of the city of Toronto, Canada. It's a giant concrete spike, with a donutlike circular deck clinging to it.

ZOOMING UP

To get up the CN Tower, you ride an elevator that travels very fast—it rises 1,122 feet (342 m) to the observation deck in just under a minute. If the tower had stories, there would be around 130 of them! When you reach the observation deck, you can go down one level to a glass floor, or visit the circular revolving restaurant upstairs.

GOING HIGHER

You can get in another elevator and go right up to the "Skypod"—a second, mini deck that's 1,465 feet (447 m) high. Up here, the tower sways in high winds.

SCARINESS

Horrifying if you don't like heights, but otherwise not too bad.

A terrifying view through the glass floor of the tower. Feel dizzy?

RACETRACK PLAYA

Racetrack Playa is a flat, dried-out lake bed in California. Dotted through it are lots of rocks, with trail-like tracks behind them, as if they've been dragged across the dry mud surface. Measurements show they move over time—yet no one has seen them do it!

STONES WITH BRAINS?

The rocks, known as "sailing stones," do really seem as if they have minds of their own. But that can't be right! People have also wondered if humans or animals are moving them. But there are no footprints or other marks in the soft lake bed. So what's really going on?

SLIPPING AND SLIDING

No one knows exactly what happens, but experts agree that it happens during early spring. The current theory is that water runs from the mountains into the playa. At night, it freezes into an "ice boat" for the rocks to float on in the dampened mud, and the rocks "sail" down a path.

SCARINESS

Stones that can wander around. Are there powerful forces at work here?

A sailing stone and the track it has made in the mud.

THAT'S AMAZING!

Some of the rocks weigh over 700 pounds (320 kg)—as much as four men.

SKELETON COAST

The Skeleton Coast sounds spooky—and it is. It's a strip of desert in Namibia, Africa, that runs along the northern part of the country's coast, and it's famous for its high death toll.

SHIPWRECKER

Shrouded in fog, with huge crashing waves and offshore rocks, the Skeleton Coast is a dangerous place for ships. In the past, hundreds of them were wrecked here. Some sailors made it ashore, but then they were in even more trouble. The breakers made it impossible to head back out to sea by boat, and the desert was barren and harsh, with little freshwater or shelter.

LOTS OF SPOOKY SKELETONS

Long ago, when whaling was common, huge whale skeletons washed up here, too. There are also around a thousand "skeletons" of old, wrecked ships—and human skeletons, belonging to the unfortunate sailors.

A spooky shipwreck lies forgotten on the coast in the Namib desert.

SCARINESS

😨 😨

Who knows what may wash up on the shore in this desert.

DID YOU KNOW? The shoreline of the Skeleton Coast is gradually changing and moving farther out to sea. That means many of the spooky shipwrecks now lie some way inland. Eerie!

HOLE OF DARVAZA

The picture on this page looks unbelievable, but it really is as it appears—a giant hole in the ground, 65 feet (20 m) deep and 195 feet (60 m) across, that's constantly glowing and burning with fire. It's near the village of Darvaza in Turkmenistan, central Asia.

DRILLING FOR GAS

The hole is a bit of a mystery, but most explanations say that engineers were searching for natural gas in this area in the 1970s. They drilled into the ground to test for gas deposits that could be tapped and sold. But when they drilled in this spot, they accidentally broke through to a vast, gas-filled underground cavern. Their drilling equipment and camping gear fell straight into it!

SET IT ABLAZE!

Some people say that the equipment set fire to the gas. Others say the engineers set the gas on fire to burn it off, which was safer than letting it waft into the village. They thought it would burn up quickly, but it's still going, decades later—probably because it's linked to a huge gas supply from underground.

DID YOU KNOW?

The name of the village, Darvaza, means "gate." That leads people to believe that the fiery hole has been there much longer—long enough for the village to be named after it.

A sightseer standing on the rim of the giant flame-filled hole.

SCARINESS

If this is a gateway into the fiery underworld, then you are better off staying far away!

GAPING GILL

Gaping Gill in Yorkshire, the United Kingdom, is a huge, 360-foot-deep (110 m) pothole—the chimneylike entrance to an underground cave system. It's on the side of a hill, and when you first see it, it looks really frightening—like a vast, dark, gaping mouth. The rocks around it are sloping and slippery, and a stream, the Fell Beck, plunges into it, too.

GOING DOWN!

Experienced cavers can rappel (see page 99) down into Gaping Gill as a way of getting into the caves connected to it, to go exploring. But every year, local caving clubs set up a scaffolding framework at the top, with a chair that is lowered by rope. Even people who have never been caving before can pay to be lowered down to the bottom.

SCARINESS

This scary, great big hole in the ground could give you claustrophobia and vertigo at the same time!

BRITAIN'S BIGGEST

Gaping Gill is one of the most famous, deepest caves in Britain. The stream that falls all 360 feet (110 m) to the bottom also forms Britain's highest unbroken waterfall.

The daunting drop down into Gaping Gill.

ST. LOUIS CEMETERY ONE

Even people who don't believe in ghosts can find graveyards scary. And this one, St. Louis Cemetery One, in New Orleans, is one of the scariest. It's said to be the most haunted cemetery in the world.

TOMBS ON TOP

In most cemeteries, the graves are underground, but not here. New Orleans is very low-lying, and the ground can be quite watery—it's a bit too soggy for graves. When people did try burying coffins, they often came floating back to the surface during a flood!

CITY OF THE DEAD

Instead, Cemetery One is full of tombs and crypts that are above ground. They look like little houses, and the coffins are stored inside. There are also rows of tombs slotted into the walls around the edges of the cemetery. This makes the cemetery look like rows of streets, so it's often called the "City of the Dead."

WHY ARE WE SCARED?

Death is a scary thought, and the idea of a ghost frightens us because it's so mysterious. There's more about them on page 66.

SCARINESS

😨 😨 😨

A seriously spooky cemetery.

WINCHESTER MYSTERY HOUSE

This crazy, supposedly haunted house in California is one of the world's weirdest buildings. It's full of winding mazes, secret rooms, doors of strange sizes, and stairs that don't lead anywhere.

THE NEVER-ENDING HOME?

The house was built in the late 1800s by a widow named Sarah Winchester, sole heir to the Winchester family fortune, which was made from selling guns like the Winchester rifle. A medium—someone who is supposed to be able to talk to the dead—advised Sarah that she was being haunted by the spirits of all those killed by Winchester guns. To keep them happy, she would have to build them a house, and keep on adding to it until she died. So she did!

SCARY SPIRITS

Sarah spent her fortune paying builders to work on the house. The dead ends and disorienting labyrinths might have been built to confuse the spirits that she was sure shared it with her. Or maybe she was following their instructions—every night, she would chat with them!

SCARINESS

More fascinating than frightening, but weird nonetheless!

If you get lost in the maze of corridors, you may never find your way out!

CHILLINGHAM CASTLE

Chilling by name, and chilling by nature . . . Chillingham Castle in Northumberland, the United Kingdom, is one of the spookiest of Britain's many medieval castles. Several ghosts are said to haunt it, and plenty of people claim to have seen and heard them—or even FELT them!

Chillingham Castle towers above its grounds—but are you brave enough to venture inside?

A GATHERING OF GHOSTS

The castle's reported ghosts include the Blue Boy—a boy in blue clothes who haunted one of the bedrooms, until a skeleton was found in one of the walls and removed. There's also Lady Mary, a lady of the castle who wanders the corridors, rustling her dress; and a strange ghost who steps out of one of the portraits on the wall and goes for a walk!

WHO WAS THAT?!

People have recounted feeling someone touch and brush against them as they were wandering around the castle's spooky rooms and dungeons. Some have also claimed they saw ghostly faces peering out at them when they looked up at the castle's windows.

SCARINESS

A spooktastically scary place!

CHAMBER OF DEATH If you really want to scare yourself, visit the torture chamber, where Scottish prisoners were held. There are instruments of torture such as eye gougers, a bed of nails, and an iron maiden (a coffinlike case filled with spikes)—and the floor was made to slope so that blood could drain away. Yuck!

LEAP CASTLE

This 500-year-old castle in Ireland has a VERY violent history. Families fought to the death over it, and many people were left to rot in the dungeons. It's said to be full of ghosts, and many people agree it has a spine-tinglingly spooky atmosphere.

THE BLOODY CHAPEL

In 1532, two brothers fought for control of the castle. One was a priest, and he was holding a service in the upper hall of the castle when his brother stormed in and stabbed him to death on the spot. The priest is said to haunt the room, now called the "Bloody Chapel," and passersby have reported seeing its windows light up at night, even when the castle is empty.

INTO THE OUBLIETTE!

There's also an oubliette, a kind of enclosed dungeon that you can't escape from. (The name, "oubliette," comes from the French word "oublier," which means "to forget.") It has spikes sticking up from the floor, and prisoners were thrown in and left to die in agony. Much later, owners had the oubliette cleared out, and found dozens of scary skeletons!

CREEPY CREATURE

Perhaps scariest of all are reports of a small, hunched, dwarflike creature with hollow eyes appearing from time to time. Those who claim to have seen it say they also smelled a horrific stench of rotting bodies.

SCARINESS

😨 😨 😨 😨

A very unnerving and creepy castle.

Leap Castle has a host of ghosts lurking inside its walls.

RAYNHAM HALL

The picture on this page is said to be a rare photograph of a real ghost, who is known as the Brown Lady of Raynham Hall. Several people have reported seeing her wafting around this stately home in Norfolk, the United Kingdom, especially on the staircase.

WHO IS THE BROWN LADY?

The ghost is said to be the spirit of Lady Dorothy Townshend, who lived in the house in the early 1700s. According to legend, her husband kept her locked up, making her so miserable that she died at age 40. She's usually described as wearing a brown dress. Sometimes she looks see-through, sometimes so solid she can be mistaken for a living person.

CAUGHT ON CAMERA

The famous photo shown here was taken in 1936, when two magazine photographers went to visit the house. One was sure he spotted a ghost on the stairs, and quickly told the other to take a picture. The other man couldn't see anything, but he photographed the stairs anyway. When the picture came out, this ghostly image appeared—so the story goes!

SCARINESS

Not the most terrifying ghost, but one of the most convincing.

WHAT DO YOU THINK?

Many ghost photos are hoaxes, made by combining two pictures. No one has proved this one is a fake, but do you think it could be?

The famous photo of the Brown Lady.

TOWER OF LONDON

This ancient castle is one of London's most famous buildings. For almost 1,000 years it's been both a royal palace and a prison, where kings and queens locked up or executed their enemies. There are countless reports of ghostly happenings here!

GHOSTS OF THE EXECUTED

Many famous figures from history lost their lives in the tower, and are now said to haunt it. They include Anne Boleyn, Henry VIII's second wife, who's said to wander around with her decapitated head under her arm! There are also the princes in the tower, 12- and 9-year-old boys who were locked up by their uncle, Richard III, so that he could protect his position on the throne. They were later murdered. People say they've seen them holding hands and crying.

SPOOKY SOUNDS AND SMELLS!

Tower guards and visitors have also heard some strange noises, such as gasping, whimpering, moaning, giggling, mysterious footsteps, and scary screams. One area, St. John's Chapel, is said to be haunted by a lady whose powerful perfume hangs around the doorway.

The Tower of London's White Tower, its most famous structure.

TOP TIP! The Tower of London is open to visitors, so you can see if you can spot any spooks yourself!

SCARINESS

A fun place to visit, with some spooky stories attached!

MUMMY TOMBS

What is a mummy? It's a dead body that hasn't rotted away. Instead of decaying until only the bones are left, it stays mostly as it is—with shrunken skin, hair, fingernails, even eyes!

TOMBS OF EGYPT

The most famous mummies were made by the ancient Egyptians. When pharaohs (kings) died, they were mummified by using saltpeter and other chemicals, and

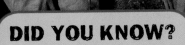

Uncannily lifelike mummies in the Palermo catacombs.

stored in stone tombs. When explorers discovered them thousands of years later, they found the bodies still strangely lifelike! Some people believe that a curse will fall on anyone who disturbs ancient Egyptian mummies.

PETRIFYING PALERMO

In Palermo, Italy, you can visit catacombs (underground tunnels) where thousands of people have been preserved after death. They're all still there, fully clothed and staring at you! Bodies were first put there around 400 years ago. They didn't rot properly, because the soil and air were so dry.

DID YOU KNOW?

Mummies can form naturally when bodies are frozen, fall into a swamp, or get stored somewhere very dry.

SCARINESS

A dead but fully preserved person can really freak you out!

MARY KING'S CLOSE

Mary King's Close is a dark, spooky underground network of streets, rooms, and passageways in Edinburgh, the United Kingdom. Many people think it's horribly haunted. You can take a guided tour through its depths to give yourself a good scare!

WHY IS IT THERE?

Edinburgh's closes are very narrow, steep streets leading downhill from the city's old main road, the Royal Mile. They run between tall, multistory houses called tenements. Most closes are open to the sky, but Mary King's Close and some others nearby were partly demolished, then covered over, in order to build a new government building in 1753. This created an eerie underground "village."

GHOSTS OF THE CLOSE

Even before it was opened to the public, Mary King's Close was said to be haunted. Today, visitors and staff claim to have seen strange shadowy shapes, and they have felt cold in some spots. They've also heard scratching coming from a chimney and the sounds of a party echoing through the gloomy chambers. Most famous is the ghost of a girl known as Annie, who is said to be searching for her lost doll. Some visitors leave her presents to cheer her up!

Can you see a ghost lurking in the shadows of this spooky close?

GHOSTLY COMPANIONS

Some staff members say there are even ghosts who follow the guided tours.

SCARINESS

Bet you wouldn't dare stay down here overnight!

SCARY MONSTERS AND STRANGE SCIENCE

The world is full of strange reports and sightings we can't quite explain—from encounters with mysterious monsters to strange, unsettling phenomena and seemingly spooky events that send a shiver down your spine! Even the world of science has strange mysteries—you'll find space-sucking black holes, freakish experiments, and potentially world-ending discoveries!

VAMPIRES

The idea of vampires is terrifying! According to legend, they're dead bodies that come to life at night, climb out of their graves, and feast on the blood of living people after biting them with their sharp fangs. And if a vampire bites you, you become one yourself! Reports of "real" vampires are rare, but their legend is all around us in movies, folklore, and fiction.

VAMPIRE MYTHS

Since ancient times, many peoples have told tales of demons or monsters that suck human blood, and "undead" bodies that get up and walk around. Over time, these myths combined. In the 1700s and 1800s, horror stories about vampires became popular, and they're still scaring us today.

VAMPIRE CULTURE

Today, vampire stories are more popular than ever, and there are thousands of vampire novels, video games, toys, cartoons, and movies.

COUNT DRACULA

In 1897, the most famous vampire book of all, Bram Stoker's *Dracula*, was published. Its vampire, Count Dracula, set much of the style for vampires as we think of them today—pale, dressed in black, strong, and able to change shape into a bat, rat, wolf, or even mist. They fear daylight and garlic, and can only be killed with a wooden stake or a silver bullet through the heart.

SCARINESS

Bloodsucking spooks that we love to be scared by!

LOCH NESS MONSTER

Do monsters really exist? If they do, the Loch Ness monster is probably one of the world's most famous. There have been reported sightings of a large, long-necked, humpbacked water creature in Loch Ness, a lake in Scotland, since medieval times.

A LIVING DINOSAUR?

Most accounts of the Loch Ness monster, or "Nessie," as it is fondly called, describe a plesiosaur, a prehistoric reptile. It has a long neck and tail, small head, oval body, and four flippers.

LOOKING AT THE EVIDENCE

The evidence for Nessie's existence includes eyewitness reports of the creature crawling around beside the loch, photos of its humps or head on the surface, and videos of a large shape moving through the water. Boats scanning the loch have also found strange shapes underwater. However, a lot of the images have turned out to be fakes, or pictures of boats or birds, on closer inspection.

SCARINESS

A mysterious lake monster sounds quite scary—but Nessie is a much-loved creature.

A famous photo claiming to show the monster of Loch Ness.

THE UNKNOWN ZOO Legendary or mysterious creatures that have not yet been proven to exist are known as cryptids, and the study of them is called cryptozoology. It means "the study of hidden animals."

CHESSIE

"Chessie," like Nessie, is a water monster supposedly seen numerous times by witnesses but never caught. It's said to live in the Chesapeake Bay, off the coast of Virginia and Maryland.

SEA SERPENT

Most reports describe the monster as very long, 30 feet (9 m), and thin with a snakelike head. Some say it has a frilly fin or "mane" down its back. In 1982, a local man named Robert Frew took a video of a serpentlike creature in the water. Experts watched the film, but couldn't decide what the animal was.

SCARINESS

The spooky sea monster that's said to look like a long, wriggly snake.

TALES FROM THE DEEP

Nessie and Chessie aren't the only mysterious sea monsters. Dozens of lakes, bays, and rivers around the world are said to have their own monsters, according to local legends.

Could a giant eel be mistaken for snaky Chessie?

YETI

"Yeti," "abominable snowman," "kang-mi," "bigfoot," "sasquatch"— this mysterious man-beast has various names. But all the reports describe something similar—a big, strong, tall, human-shaped creature that walks upright like a person but is covered in thick hair like a bear. In some places, these creatures are said to attack and eat people; in others, they're supposedly shy and hide away.

MOUNTAIN MAN

Most reports of these scary, hairy monsters come from very remote high mountain and forest areas, such as the Himalayas and the Rocky Mountains. That would explain why no one has ever caught one or found a dead one, and why they are so hard to spot. If they're real, that is!

SCARINESS

Based on the size of some yeti footprints that have been found, you wouldn't want to be caught in a yeti's path!

The "bigfoot" filmed in 1967— or was it a man in a costume?

BIGFOOT ON FILM In 1967, a yeti hunter claimed to have caught a bigfoot on camera in California. His footage documents the most famous sighting to this day. It has often been called a hoax, and debate rages over whether it's real.

CHUPACABRA

The name "chupacabra" means "goatsucker." It's a mysterious beast that has been reported in the Americas, where people claim it kills goats and other farm animals and pets by sucking their blood. But what exactly is it supposed to look like?

HOPPING DOG

In some reports, the chupacabra is a cross between a wild dog and a kangaroo. It has sharp doglike fangs, but hops around on its back legs. Whenever anyone claimed to have caught and killed one, however, it turned out to be a coyote (a type of wild dog) with its fur and skin damaged by a disease called mange. Unpleasant, but not a monster!

SPIKY ALIEN

Around 1995, a series of sightings gave the chupacabra a very different look. It was described as a two-legged, human-shaped creature with lizardlike skin, spikes down its back, and glowing red eyes!

MOVIE MONSTER

Eventually, people noticed that the description of the lizardlike chupacabra was strangely similar to "Sil," a creature with glowing red eyes from a sci-fi movie released in 1995.

SCARINESS

This infamous beast is scarily sinister!

GHOSTS

Most people know someone who claims to have seen a ghost. People love to tell ghost stories and scare one another with unearthly tales. Ghosts are said to dwell in spooky houses, castles, and graveyards—like the ones in this book—all over the world.

WHAT IS A GHOST?

Most people think of a ghost as the spirit of a person (or animal) who has died. Ghosts are usually said to linger on in this world for a reason, and haunt the place where they used to live. They can appear to people, moan, talk, or make strange noises. Some people even say they've felt a ghost grab them!

HARD TO PIN DOWN

It is hard to prove the existence of ghosts. Even in the most haunted of places, ghosts will not appear on demand. They seem to come and go, and are hard to catch on camera. There are photos of ghosts, but it's pretty hard to tell if they're genuine.

Ghosts aren't just found in spooky old buildings.

SCARINESS

Whether or not ghosts are searching for something, or someone, it is certainly creepy to think about bumping into them.

EXPLANATIONS

No one really knows what causes ghostly sightings. It could be that surroundings can somehow "record" and play back past events. Or ghosts could be explained by dreams or hallucinations.

POLTERGEISTS

A poltergeist is a mysterious, ghostlike presence that's said to make objects move, crash, and clatter about. Sometimes, according to reports, they even pick up people and fling them across the room! However, some people say a poltergeist is actually a kind of telekinesis (see page 73).

WHAT HAPPENS?

In most poltergeist reports, the haunting isn't so much linked to a place but to a person. Wherever the poltergeist goes, things start moving around and breaking, there are mysterious noises, and strange messages may appear. The poltergeist may stay for a few weeks or months, but usually goes away eventually.

STRESSED AND SPOOKY

Some researchers who have tried to investigate poltergeist reports say that the person who is haunted is usually someone who's unhappy or stressed. They think the strange effects could be caused by some kind of electric field or force coming from the person's mind.

A poltergeist can hurl objects around a room, throw things at you—or even move furniture.

SCARINESS

😨 😨 😨 😨

...ries of these noisy, destructive ghosts can be really scary!

THE ROSENHEIM POLTERGEIST

One famous example happened in Rosenheim, Germany. The poltergeist followed a woman named Annemarie Schneider, making objects move and creating strange sounds in her office.

WITCHES

What is a witch? Traditionally, a witch was a woman (or sometimes a man) who people believed could cast magic spells—either to heal the sick or to harm people with curses!

WITCH HUNTS

If someone was accused of being a witch, they could be tortured or put to death. This often happened in Europe and the United States in the past, and similar things still happen today in some countries where people believe in magic and witchcraft.

BLACK HATS AND BROOMSTICKS

Today, you can dress up as a witch on Halloween, with a black, pointy hat and cloak and a broomstick to ride. This idea of what a witch looks like comes from old fairy tales, and there are hundreds of fictional witches in books—many of them funny, not frightening.

SCARINESS

Witches can be scary, but being accused of being a witch is even worse!

The most famous witch trials occurred in Salem, Massachusetts, in 1692.

WITCH TRIALS? People used to be "tested" to see whether they were witches. One way was to throw them into water with their hands and feet tied. If they sank and drowned, they were innocent. If they floated, they had to be executed. Not very fair either way!

ALIENS

We're so used to seeing fake aliens on TV and in movies, it's easy to forget that in real life, we don't actually know much about what they might be like. An alien could be a humanoid like us, a tiny germ, or perhaps something we can't even imagine.

IS LIFE LIKELY?

What are the chances of life beyond our planet? They're actually pretty high. In 1991, astronomers discovered exoplanets—planets outside our solar system—and now we know there are hundreds of them. Some have the right temperature and conditions for life to exist, placing them in what's known as the "Goldilocks zone" (because it's just right!). The universe is so big, there are probably billions of planets where life could exist.

ALARMING ALIENS

Imagine you woke up tomorrow to hear the news that an alien species had contacted us. It would be incredibly exciting! If we do discover aliens, we just have to hope they're friendly—they might want to invade Earth!

Some people believe that aliens have already visited our planet. See page 71.

See page 71.

SCARINESS

If there are aliens out there, they might be scary!

MAKING CONTACT

Astronomers watch for any interesting signals from space that could be an alien message. We have also sent probes out into space with pictures and sound recordings of Earth for anyone out there to find.

UFOS

The word "UFO" makes us think of alien spaceships, but actually it just stands for "unidentified flying object." So most UFOs are probably planes, satellites, weather balloons, or other earthly creations. Still, plenty of people are sure that alien spacecraft do visit our planet.

SAUCERS AND SPACE TRIPS

There have been hundreds of sightings of saucer-shaped flying objects like the one on this page. Of course, many could be fakes—for example, someone could throw a round object such as a lamp shade or hubcap into the sky while someone else photographs it.

SCARINESS

There are plenty of strange lights the night sky—could they be invad alien spaceships?

IT'S A COVER-UP!

If aliens had visited us, surely we would all know about it by now, as it would have been widely reported and studied. That suggests there's little real evidence. But UFO fanatics claim that governments don't want us to find out about aliens, so they hide the facts and cover up the proof. Or maybe the aliens themselves are being secretive.

STRANGE SIGHTS

Throughout history, there have been strange accounts of UFOs. They're often described as round or oval, glowing with light, and flying at impossible speeds.

A mysterious view of a flying saucer.

ALIEN ABDUCTIONS

Some people have reported amazing experiences of being abducted (kidnapped) by alien spaceships. The trouble is, it's impossible to prove one person's account, and stories like these are pretty easy to dream, hallucinate, or even make up completely!

BETTY AND BARNEY

One of the most famous and earliest "abductions" happened in 1961, to a couple named Betty and Barney Hill. They were driving home from vacation when they saw a bright light in the sky, which came closer and appeared to be a spaceship. After that, the two didn't remember anything—they found themselves farther down the road two hours later. But gradually, they remembered being taken aboard the ship and meeting small gray "alien" beings who asked them questions and did strange tests on them.

ME, TOO!

Experts have noticed that abductees' stories often follow a similar pattern. This suggests people could be copying earlier stories, or maybe hallucinating!

Many people around the world claim to have been "beamed up" into an alien spaceship.

GALACTIC TOURISM

If you are ever abducted by aliens, try to bring back some alien technology as a souvenir. Strangely, no one has managed to do this yet!

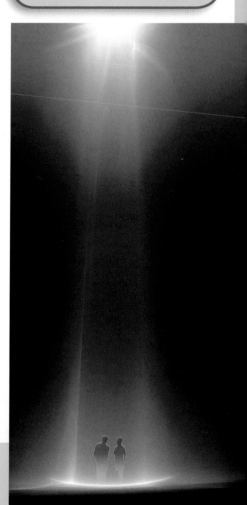

SCARINESS

Being kidnapped by aliens for their experiments would scare anyone!

MIND READING AND ESP

Can you and your friends send messages using just your minds?
If ESP, or extrasensory perception, really works, you could.

BEYOND THE SENSES

Extrasensory perception means being able to sense things with our minds instead of with our normal senses. It includes telepathy (sending and receiving mind messages) and being able to "see" something that's happening far away or in the future.

IS IT REAL?

Many people think there is some truth to ESP—yet when scientists try to test it, it's hard to find evidence. Most people say they sometimes get a "sixth sense" about something. The phone rings and you just know who it is, or you get a funny feeling something's going to go wrong. But scientists say these could be coincidences.

PSYCHIC POWERS

Some people claim to be psychic with powers such as ESP, but they find it hard to prove this in scientific tests. Do you believe them?

SCARINESS

Could somebody read your thought

This man is trying to use ESP to read the woman's mind.

TELEKINESIS

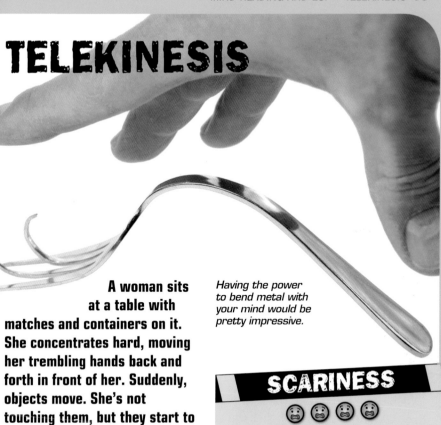

Having the power to bend metal with your mind would be pretty impressive.

A woman sits at a table with matches and containers on it. She concentrates hard, moving her trembling hands back and forth in front of her. Suddenly, objects move. She's not touching them, but they start to shift and slide, inching toward her. Pretty spooky to watch!

SCARINESS

😨 😨 😨 😨

If some people can move objects with their minds, what else can they do?

MIND MOVEMENT

This demonstration of telekinesis (movement using the mind) took place in Russia in 1967. The woman was Nina Kulagina, who claimed to be able to make things move with just the power of her mind. She said it took a huge amount of effort and concentration.

A USEFUL SKILL!

If telekinesis was easy, we'd all be doing it, wouldn't we? You wouldn't have to go to the kitchen for a snack—you'd just command it to sail through the air to you!

DID YOU KNOW? Another type of telekinesis is changing the shape of objects. This was made famous by a performer named Uri Geller, who often appeared on TV in the 1970s and 1980s, bending spoons and forks.

BERMUDA TRIANGLE

In the Atlantic Ocean, close to Florida and the Caribbean Sea, is an imaginary triangle, thought to be 500,000 square miles (800,000 square km), notorious for the number of ships and planes that have been lost there. Besides the crashes and shipwrecks, some craft have simply disappeared without a trace.

WHERE DID THEY GO?

There have been all kinds of weird and supernatural explanations for what happens in the Bermuda Triangle. Have the missing ships and planes been sucked into space, grabbed by aliens or sea monsters, or dragged into a time-travel portal? Or maybe they were destroyed by powerful supernatural or magnetic forces from the mythical sunken land of Atlantis?

HANG ON A MINUTE . . . !

Unfortunately, the Bermuda Triangle isn't as mysterious as you might think (though it can be dangerous). There are certainly a lot of accidents and disappearances. But this is also one of the busiest sea and air routes in the world—so there are plenty of ships and planes passing through it. It's also a hot spot for hurricanes and other storms. So the accident rate is hardly surprising!

SCARINESS

Beware of flying through here!

BERMUDA BUBBLES

Scientists have also found gas deposits in the seabed that could possibly bubble up to the surface. This would make the sea frothy and foamy, swallowing ships up. But there's no hard evidence it has ever happened.

A giant waterspout in the Bermuda Triangle appears without warning.

CROP CIRCLES

Since the 1970s, the peculiar phenomenon of crop circles has become increasingly common, and spread around the world. Crop circles are intricate shapes and pictures (not always just plain circles) that appear in fields. Often crop circles appear overnight, as if by magic—some people believe they are made by aliens.

IT WAS ME!

Plenty of people have come forward to say that they make crop circles themselves, marking out a design using planks attached to ropes to flatten the crops. Teams of crop circle makers compete to make the neatest, most beautiful patterns.

NO, IT WASN'T!

However, supporters of the alien theory say these trampled circles are just fakes and copies, but the "real things" still exist. Real crop circles, they claim, form as crop stalks heat up and bend suddenly, instead of being flattened by planks. Some people say they have seen strange unidentified lights darting around above the field as the circle is being created.

FREAK STORMS?

Some scientists have proposed the patterns are caused by wind or lightning, but this hasn't been proved.

An amazing crop circle—but what could it mean?

SCARINESS

Are they really messages from other worlds?

SPACEWALKING

Spacewalking isn't really walking, since you're not on the ground! It means going out into space on your own, instead of staying inside a spacecraft. Astronauts often do it when they have to make repairs or replace spacecraft parts.

WHAT TO WEAR

Of course, you can't simply wander into space unprotected, as there's no oxygen and no air pressure. In this vacuum, you couldn't breathe, you would lose consciousness, and your skin would swell. So spacewalkers need a helmet, an oxygen supply, and a full space suit that recreates the air pressure on Earth.

ARGH! I'M FLOATING AWAY

The scariest thing about a space walk is that if you got separated from your space vehicle, you could just float away . . . FOREVER! When an astronaut leaves a spacecraft, they're both moving in the same direction, but a bump or spin could send the walker hurtling away.

Edward White was the first American to step outside his spacecraft.

WALKING THE WALK

A space walk can take several hours, so a space suit has a built-in drink holder and even a diaper!

SCARINESS

😨 😨

Spacewalking must be an amazing feeling—but a malfunction would be terrifying.

BLACK HOLES

A black hole in space has no volume, only mass. That means it contains a huge amount of matter (stuff), so it's very heavy and has powerful gravity. The black hole's gravity is so strong it sucks in anything that gets close enough. Black holes even suck in light (which is how they got their name).

WHY DON'T THEY SUCK IN EVERYTHING?

Black holes sound pretty terrifying—as if they could devour the whole universe. But this doesn't happen. Just like a planet, such as Earth, a black hole's gravity is strong when you're close to it, but if you're far enough away, it won't affect you. Luckily for us, there are no black holes nearby.

A BLACK HOLE ON EARTH?

Scientists sometimes study matter by smashing tiny particles, using a particle accelerator such as the Large Hadron Collider located between France and Switzerland. Some people are afraid that this could actually create a black hole that could swallow Earth. But most scientists don't agree with this!

Scientists believe that a black hole is strong enough to tear apart a star, and then swallow it up!

SCARINESS

😨

Being sucked into a black hole would be horrifying. Luckily, it's unlikely!

PORTALS TO OTHER TIMES

In sci-fi stories, black holes can create time-travel tunnels or lead to other universes.

KILLER VIRUSES

A virus is a type of germ that invades body cells and makes you sick. They can spread from one person to another. Flu, HIV, the common cold, and measles are all examples of diseases caused by viruses.

A lethal avian flu virus.

GERM RACE

We have medicines that can treat most of these illnesses. The trouble is, viruses change. They can combine or mutate to make new versions. This means viruses can suddenly become much more deadly, or a new virus can appear. Eventually, a virus could develop that's both very deadly and very easily passed between people. It could spread around the globe and kill millions or even billions (called a pandemic).

SCARINESS

Could a deadly virus wipe us all ou

VIRUSES NEED LIFE

However, viruses need humans in order to survive! They cannot reproduce unless they attach themselves to a living cell.

FEARFUL FLU The flu (short for influenza) can be a mild disease, or it can be deadly. This virus is probably the most likely to cause a pandemic, as it mutates so fast. But scientists are working hard to make vaccines to protect us.

GENETIC ENGINEERING

Genes are the tiny sets of instructions inside the cells of all living things that tell our bodies how to work. Genetic engineering means making changes to genes.

YIKES! LIKE WHAT?

At the moment, genetically engineered creatures aren't THAT scary. They include things like strawberry plants with a gene added from a deep-sea fish. The gene stops them from freezing during frosty weather by making a natural antifreeze chemical. But using the same technology, we could make scarier combinations, such as a creature that's half human and half animal, or extra-dangerous germs.

DESIGNER CREATURES

Eventually, we may even be able to design our own life-forms, by putting together a whole new genome (set of genes). Imagine real monsters being made!

SCARINESS

Could scientists really design monsters, or create killer germs?

A protein from a glowing jellyfish has made the mouse glow this eerie green color under UV light.

USEFUL GENETIC ENGINEERING

So far, genetic engineering has been mainly helpful, allowing us to create stronger crops and engineer bacteria for useful medicines. However, many people are scared of it because of where it could lead. Others are worried that foods made this way could be bad for us.

NANOTECHNOLOGY

"Nano" means "one billionth," or something very, very tiny. So nanotechnology is technology on a tiny scale. It means making machines by joining tiny parts. Sometimes, the machines themselves are tiny, too.

WHAT COULD IT DO?

There are lots of amazing possible uses for nanotechnology. We might have our own "nanofactories" at home that could build any product we like. Tiny, invisible machines could clean up pollution, or enter the body to destroy diseases and mend damage. Maybe we could even build food instead of having to grow it.

WHY IS IT SCARY?

The trouble is, things like this could be very dangerous in the wrong hands. Criminals and terrorists could use nanofactories to make bombs or poisons. Like a nightmarish sci-fi movie!

A nanomachine could be programmed to destroy a cancer cell in the human body.

SCARINESS

Nanotechnology could be useful, or go horribly wrong!

GRAY GOO Another fear is that tiny, supersmart nano robots, or "nanobots," could take over the earth! If they could find their own fuel and replicate themselves, they could multiply over and over, making a vast mass of artificial life known as "gray goo."

ARTIFICIAL INTELLIGENCE

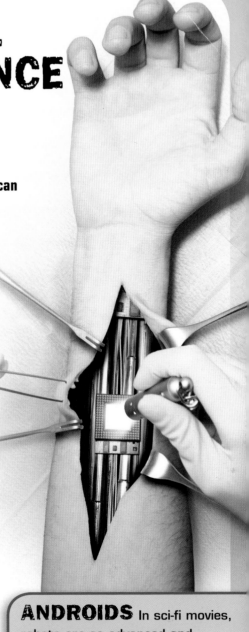

Artificial intelligence (AI) is technology that recreates the abilities of real-life brains: robots that can sense their surroundings and respond, and computers that can make decisions or have a lifelike "conversation" with you.

THINKING MACHINES

Computers are quickly getting more and more powerful. Some experts predict that a point will come when artificial intelligence will become "superintelligence" and overtake human abilities. It hasn't happened yet, though you can find it in plenty of sci-fi films.

MACHINES IN CONTROL

In the scariest futuristic visions, superintelligent robots could figure out how to build newer, smarter machines, and find their own power supply. They wouldn't need humans anymore, and could even start to control us.

One day, we could make completely human-looking robots!

SCARINESS

bots are pretty cool—unless they decide to take over the world.

ANDROIDS In sci-fi movies, robots are so advanced and lifelike, they look completely human and you can't tell the difference. Could this ever really happen? Possibly. Scientists are already working on realistic fake skin and facial expressions that mimic human emotions.

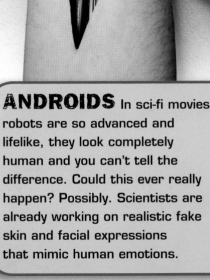

SCARY STUNTS AND FRIGHTENING FEATS

The great outdoors can be a very scary place! It may be easy enough to summon the courage to ride a roller coaster or even bungee jump. But other feats, such as wing walking or cliff diving, are much more terrifying. Gather your strength and read on to discover more daring outdoor adventures!

STUNT FLYING

Planes aren't just for getting from A to B. They can also perform astonishing stunts that show off the pilot's skill, or make you think the plane is definitely going to crash—before it swoops to safety at the last minute.

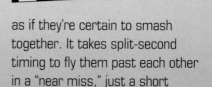

SHOW-OFFS

You can often see stunt flying, also called aerobatics, at air shows or in aerobatic displays put on for special occasions. Often a show will include teams performing stunts—it is terrifying to see two planes whoosh toward each other as if they're certain to smash together. It takes split-second timing to fly them past each other in a "near miss," just a short distance apart.

STUNTS TO SEE

- Loop-the-loop: Flying up, over, and around in a full circle.
- Roll: Turning the plane over as it flies forward.
- Stall turn: Flying straight up until the plane almost stops—then dropping back down.
- Swoop: Flying low to the ground.

CRASH! One of the most effective stunts is imitating an accident to scare the crowds! The plane seems to stall and tumble, spinning in every direction. The pilot may trail fake smoke as well. Then, at the last minute, the pilot takes control again.

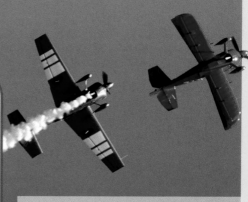

A stunt team in action, using smoke to track their paths.

WING WALKING

When you wing walk, you're strapped to the top of a small plane as it climbs, circles, loops-the-loop, and swoops close to the ground. It's literally hair raising! You thunder along at up to 160 mph (260 km/h), with the wind blasting into your face.

WALKING WHERE?

"Wing walking" is a strange name for it, as you don't actually wander up and down on the plane's wings. If you tried that, you'd soon be blown off and end up back on the ground! Instead, there's a special frame on the plane for you to lean on, and you have a harness to hold you in place. However, professional wing walkers do change position and perform acrobatic moves such as handstands.

WHERE CAN I SEE IT?

Today, the best way to see wing walkers is to go to an air show, where they are often part of the entertainment. Sometimes there are two or more planes, each with its own wing walker, flying in formation and performing tricks.

WOMEN WING WALKERS The best wing walkers are lightweight women. Size is important so the plane won't overbalance.

SCARINESS

Not for anyone scared of flying!

A wing walker performing high in the sky.

STUNT DRIVING

High-speed chases and races, driving through crowded markets, crashing, flipping and rolling, smashing through barriers, and jumping over big gaps all feature in lots of movies.

STUNT SCHOOL

You can actually go to a special film-driving school to learn to be a stunt driver. As well as being a great driver, you need to be calm and controlled—NOT a crazy daredevil! It's also good to be quite small. You'll roll around and hit your head less during crashes and tricks, and it also makes the cars look bigger and more powerful. Whatever you do, though, you'll get cuts, bruises, aches, and pains from crash landings—stunt drivers do risk their lives for their work.

THE NEED FOR SPEED

The car chase is a big set piece in many thriller, crime, and action movies. Audiences love seeing cars do stunts in dangerous locations or famous urban settings. Skilled stunt drivers are an essential part of the film and TV industry.

A daredevil driver at the International Stunt Festival in Belgrade, Serbia.

IN SAFE HANDS

With all their training and experience crashing and chasing, stunt drivers actually make better and safer drivers!

SCARINESS

Being a stunt driver is a thrilling but pretty frightening job.

SKYDIVING

Being high up is scary because of the frightening feeling that you could fall. But when you're skydiving, you DO fall! You jump out of a plane and plunge straight down, zooming toward the ground faster than a sprinting cheetah. Luckily, of course, you do have a parachute.

FALLING FOR FUN

Parachutes were first invented in the 1400s, and developed as a way of getting down from a height safely. Later on, they were also used to drop soldiers into war zones. After the 1940s, though, leaping out of planes became more of a hobby. People say the sense of danger is exhilarating.

SCARINESS

😨 😨 😨 😨

Terrifying—but you'd only do it if you liked it!

DEATH-DEFYING FEATS

A skydiver normally jumps from a plane about 13,000 feet (4,000 m) up. They have a minute or so of free fall before having to open their chute. In that time, they can perform tricks such as somersaults, or fall in formation with other skydivers. This can be more dangerous, as people can crash into one another or get distracted and open their chutes too late.

Skydivers make their death-defying leaps from a plane.

SPEEDING BULLET Extra-crazy skydivers try to go as fast as they can by falling headfirst, with their bodies in a streamlined bullet shape. They can fall at up to 330 mph (480 km/h).

WINGSUIT FLYING

Humans have conquered the air with flying machines—planes, balloons, and helicopters. But what if you could actually fly with your own wings? Wingsuit flying is one of the closest things we have to that. It means skydiving wearing a special suit that has "wings" between the arms and body, and between the legs.

PERMISSION TO LAND

A wingsuit has a parachute backpack built into it for landing. But wingsuit makers are trying to develop a suit that you can land in safely without a chute.

WHAT HAPPENS?

When you jump out of a plane wearing a wingsuit, you'll fall much more slowly than normal. The wings of the suit fill with air as you fall, and work like real wings, allowing you to glide forward. You can soar, swoop, and loop-the-loop. You can also fly a long way—some wingsuit divers have flown almost 12.5 miles (20 km) horizontally in a single skydive.

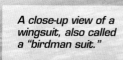

A close-up view of a wingsuit, also called a "birdman suit."

DID YOU KNOW?

The modern wingsuit was invented in the 1990s by French skydiver Patrick de Gayardon. Unfortunately, a parachute malfunction led to his death in 1998.

SCARINESS

😨 😨 😨 😨

This extreme sport takes a lot of guts.

BASE JUMPING

BASE jumping is parachuting, but without a plane. Jumpers leap from something fixed to the ground. The letters "BASE" stand for "building," "antenna" (a tall tower or radio mast), "span" (a bridge), and "earth" (a naturally high cliff or mountain).

A BASE jumper leaps from a terrifyingly high cliff.

GET IT RIGHT

Maybe you think parachuting from a building or bridge would be less scary than falling 13,000 feet (4,000 m) from a plane. You'd be wrong! The reason BASE jumping is so risky is that there's no margin for error. There's only a very short time to open your parachute before you hit the ground. There's often not much space to land in. And because you're falling close to cliffs or buildings, a gust of wind can cause a deadly crash.

DEADLY HOBBY

Early parachutists tried a few daring jumps from cliffs and towers, but modern BASE jumping really took off in the 1970s. It was made popular by Norwegian skydiving photographer Carl Boenish. What happened to him? Unfortunately, he died on a BASE jump in Norway in 1984. This sport has sadly claimed a long list of lives.

RISKY LEAPERS BASE jumpers sometimes leap from structures as low as 112 feet (34 m). Falling from that height to the ground only takes about 2.6 seconds!

SCARINESS

One of the scariest sports on Earth—even if you're only watchin

SKI JUMPING

Ski jumping is an Olympic sport, but when you think about what it involves, it's pretty crazy! After hurtling down a giant icy ramp at speeds of up to 60 mph (100 km/h), a ski jumper can fly 390 feet (120 m) or more through the air, soaring up to 60 feet (18 m) above the ground. Rocketing through the air like that would normally mean a very nasty, and probably deadly, landing.

HOW DO THEY DO IT?

Ski jumpers usually remain unscathed because they land on a slope, lining their skis up with it as they touch down. It takes a LOT of skill to get the flight exactly right and land smoothly. You couldn't start by whizzing down an Olympic-size ski slope and then seeing what happened. To train, often when they're still children, ski jumpers start with little jumps, and gradually build up to the big ones.

IS IT DANGEROUS?

Ski jumpers can die while jumping, usually from landing badly, falling, and hitting their heads or necks. But this is rare. Ski jumping is actually no more dangerous than some other winter sports, such as snowboarding.

SCARINESS

😨 😨

It looks petrifying, but professional ski jumpers know what they're doing.

A competitive ski jumper launches himself through the sky.

BIGGEST JUMPS Ski jumpers are scored on how far they fly not how high. In long-distance ski jumping, known as ski flying, jumpers can leap 650 feet (200 m)—the length of seven basketball courts!

BUILDERING

The more skyscrapers are built, the more exciting challenges there are for a builderer, or urban climber! These death-defying daredevils like to climb up the OUTSIDE of the highest buildings they can—often with no ropes or safety equipment at all.

HOLDING ON

There are thousands of tall buildings around the world, with all kinds of cool decorative designs. Some have bars, ledges, or pipework on them that make the climb fairly easy. Others are so sleek and smooth, it's amazing that anyone can climb them. Top builderers are very strong and light, and can hold on by pushing their fingers into tiny crevices.

HEY! GET OFF MY BUILDING!

Builderers can get permission to do a climb. But there are a few, such as famous French builderer Alain Robert, who break the law by climbing on private buildings, against the owners' wishes. As well as risking their own lives, they can cause havoc in city centers as a crowd gathers to watch. The police have to clear a space around the building so they don't land on anyone if they fall off. Then the police arrest the climbers once they get to the top.

SCARINESS

Hanging off the outside of a skyscraper must be petrifying!

Builderer Alain Robert, nicknamed Spiderman, climbs the Federation Tower in Moscow, Russia.

THE HUMAN FLY

Unlike some extreme sports, buildering isn't new. An American, George Polley, was nicknamed the Human Fly for climbing hundreds of high buildings from 1910 to 1927.

FREE RUNNING

Free running is a strange hobby. It involves running, jumping, swinging, and backflipping around city structures and obstacles. A slip can be bad news. It takes a lot of skill, practice, and, more importantly, courage to do it well.

BREATHTAKING LEAPS

Top free runners can do some amazing stunts, like running straight up a wall into a backflip, jumping all the way down a flight of steps in one go, or even leaping huge gaps between buildings. They are superfit and do lots of training, so they know how to land safely and avoid injuries. Inexperienced free runners often get into trouble trying to imitate professional moves!

This fearless free runner launches himself over an impressive gap.

RUNNING WITH STYLE

Free running grew out of parkour, which developed in France around 1990. Parkour is about trying to get from A to B efficiently and smoothly, making use of obstacles along the way. In free running, runners add their own style by doing cool-looking moves—acrobatic jumps and twists, somersaults, slides, and flips—sometimes in formation with other runners.

WATCH IT!

To really grasp free running, look on the Web for a video of a leading free runner, such as Sébastien Foucan.

SCARINESS

Some free running moves look superhuman.

SKIN DIVING

Skin diving, or free diving, is the extreme sport of diving without diving gear or breathing equipment—usually to see who can go the deepest and then safely return to the surface.

HOW IS IT POSSIBLE?

As you may know, if you want to dive deep underwater, you normally need breathing equipment such as scuba gear. This is because below a certain depth, water pressure presses your chest in, so your lungs can't expand. Diving gear pushes compressed air into your lungs to solve this problem. Skin divers dive as deep as or deeper than most scuba divers, where the water pressure is huge. They do this by simply not breathing at all while underwater.

HOLD YOUR BREATH

Most people can't hold their breath for long—half a minute, or a minute maybe. Top skin divers can manage deepwater dives that take a mind-blowing FOUR minutes.

Audrey Mestre, a French free diver, breaks the world record.

SCARINESS

Being deep underwater and unable to breathe is seriously scary!

WATER LUNGS

When we dive, our lungs fill with blood plasma (the watery part of blood) to keep them from being crushed. This is a natural mammalian reflex that all humans have.

CLIFF DIVING

Imagine standing right on the edge of a cliff, in nothing but your swimming gear! You are headed 85 feet (26 m) below (that's as high as an eight-story apartment building). This is what cliff divers do at spectacular locations around the world—in competitions, or just for fun!

SPLASH!

Diving off a high cliff means hitting the water at high speed—up to 62 mph (100 km/h) at the moment of impact. You might think water makes a soft landing, but at those speeds it can do serious damage and feel as hard as rock. Divers have to be very fit and strong, and perfect their technique so that they can enter the water smoothly and safely. No belly flops!

LOOK AT MEEEE!

The best cliff divers put on a show with spins, twists, and poses on the way down. Sometimes two or three divers do a synchronized dive.

SCARINESS

Leaping off a cliff is not only dangerous—but terrifying, too!

The path of a cliff diver's graceful, somersaulting dive.

CAVING

Deep under the ground we walk around on every day are millions of passageways, caverns, and underground rivers. Exploring this dark, damp world is an exciting hobby—unless you get lost, stuck, or swept away!

INTO THE CAVES

Cave systems can stretch for huge distances underground, with lots of chambers linked by narrow tunnels. In some places, caves open out onto the surface, and that's where cavers get in. They have to be very careful to remember exactly where they're going, so that they can find their way back out. Cavers also need helmets, waterproof flashlights, spare batteries, warm clothes, and emergency rations, in case they do get lost.

A caver braves a narrow gap.

SCARINESS

Caving can be easy and fun—or nightmarishly claustrophobic.

WATCH OUT FOR THE WATER

Because caves are below ground, water from the surface collects there. There are some stunning underground pools and waterfalls, and some cavers—called cave divers—actually explore water-filled caves by swimming through them. After heavy rain, caves can flood quickly, so they have to be careful!

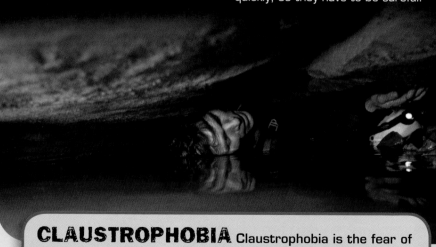

CLAUSTROPHOBIA

Claustrophobia is the fear of small, enclosed spaces. Cavers sometimes have to squeeze through tiny gaps—not ideal for a claustrophobe!

ROLLER COASTER

Everyone knows what a roller coaster is—but not everyone has been on one. That's because they're too scary! On the other hand, some people love the thrill of a roller coaster ride—and the more terrifying, the better.

WAYS TO SCARE YOU

A good roller coaster is safe and strong, but built to scare the living daylights out of you. The coaster cars roll along a track, but they're often wider than the track so that you can't see it and it seems as if you're flying. Turning a sharp corner makes you feel like you'll be flung off into space. The cars climb slowly up huge "hills," then plummet down the other side at breakneck speed. Many coasters have corkscrew twists that turn you completely upside down.

SCARINESS

Roller coaster fans travel the world in order to try out the most thrilling rides.

GET IN!

On some rides, you hang beneath the rail with your legs dangling; on others, you ride standing up (but still strapped in!).

Visitors zoom around on a roller coaster at a park at LaQua, Japan.

BOBSLEDDING

Even sledding down a snowy hill can be a bit scary, if you go very fast. The Olympic sport of bobsledding is much scarier! The sled shoots down a specially made tubelike track.

OFF WE GO!

Though a bobsled can reach bone-shakingly fast speeds of up to 100 mph (160 km/h), it has no engine. It's powered by nothing more than gravity—and a good push off. The team starts by running alongside, pushing the sled, then jumps in as it speeds up. The person at the front steers, aiming to take the fastest, smoothest course around the corners, while avoiding a nasty crash into a solid ice wall.

SCARY SKELETON

There are even more dangerous versions of the sport. A bob skeleton is a tiny, traylike sled that you ride lying facedown on your stomach. You hurtle along just inches from the solid ice at up to 80 mph (130 km/h).

SCARINESS

One of the most thrilling and nail-biting winter sports.

The German bobsled team zooms down a track in the 2008 Winter Olympics.

BUNGEE JUMPING

If you go bungee jumping, a long, stretchy bungee cord is attached to your body or feet using a special harness. Then you step to the edge of the drop, and . . . jump! You go into free fall until you start stretching the elastic. It makes you slow down, stop, and then bounce up and down a few more times. Making the leap takes guts, even though you're tied on.

BOING!
The idea for bungee jumping probably came from the "land diving" tradition of Vanuatu, an island nation in the South Pacific.

There, young men leap from 100-foot (30 m) high wooden towers, using vines tied to their legs to stop them from hitting the ground. They do it as a test of courage and manhood. In the 1970s, extreme sports fans decided to try out a modern version, using elasticized rope. They made their first jumps from Clifton Suspension Bridge in Bristol, the United Kingdom.

GIANT JUMPS
Stuntman Dave Barlia did one of the highest-ever bungee jumps in 2001, jumping from a helicopter 10,000 feet (3,300 m) up in the air!

SCARINESS

Free falling and bouncing in the air is some people's nightmare!

A bold bungee jumper.

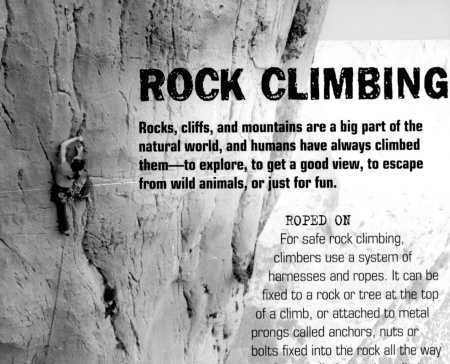

ROCK CLIMBING

Rocks, cliffs, and mountains are a big part of the natural world, and humans have always climbed them—to explore, to get a good view, to escape from wild animals, or just for fun.

ROPED ON

For safe rock climbing, climbers use a system of harnesses and ropes. It can be fixed to a rock or tree at the top of a climb, or attached to metal prongs called anchors, nuts or bolts fixed into the rock all the way up. As you climb, another climber, the belayer, tightens the rope so that if you do slip, you don't have far to fall. Climbing this way is pretty safe, if you're doing it properly. But people can still get so scared by how high up they are that they freeze and have to be helped down!

EXTREME CLIMBERS

Of course, some climbers seek the freedom of climbing without ropes. Some top rock climbers go "free soloing"—climbing high, dangerous routes with no ropes at all. Just watching them is enough to have you sweating and trembling. And of course, it's NOT something you should ever try.

A NIGHT ON THE ROCK
Climbing a really big rock face can take a few days! Overnight, climbers sleep in sleeping bags on a ledge, tied firmly to the cliff face. Sweet dreams!

This adventurous climber scales Verdon Gorge, in France.

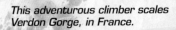

SCARINESS

Ranges from exciting to gut-churning terror!

RAPPELLING

Rappelling, also called abseiling, is a way of getting down to the ground safely from somewhere high up by using a rope. Rock climbers use it to return to the ground. Window cleaners and miners sometimes rappel for their jobs.

HOW IT WORKS

When you're rappelling, the rope is looped and knotted in a special way so that you can let it run through your hand and control how fast you go down. Usually, there's also a belayer in charge of the rope to keep you safe (see opposite).

OVER YOU GO!

The scariest part comes first, as once you're roped up, you have to lower yourself backward over the edge and drop into position. When rappelling down a cliff face, you can push against it with your feet and "bunny hop" to the bottom. For this, you have to position your feet wide apart and push off with them both—otherwise you can end up spinning around and hitting your head.

SCARINESS

carily high, but easy to do—and at least you're heading down to solid ground!

A climber rappels from a great height after a climb.

TRAPPED! Rappelling with long hair can be bad news, as it can get caught in the ropes! Keep it tied up.

WHITE-WATER RAFTING

A white-water raft is a large, inflatable boat, used for zooming along a rushing river while carrying a load of passengers.

SCARINESS

Lots of fun, but sometimes scary and dangerous.

WHAT IS WHITE WATER?

White water is river water that's flowing fast over shallows, rocks, and waterfalls, making it frothy and foamy. It's fun to raft on because it's so fast and bumpy, but it's also dangerous if you fall in—you could be swept away by a strong current.

A GREAT DAY OUT

This extreme sports activity is popular around the world—you can do it without much training at all, and a lot of people try it on vacation. The boat usually holds up to 12 people, and you sit along the sides. You have to wear a life jacket and a helmet, and each person gets an oar to help control the raft. On a good, fast-flowing river, it's a thrilling, noisy, high-speed ride, bouncing along over rocks, rapids, and mini-waterfalls while clinging on tight and getting soaked by the spray.

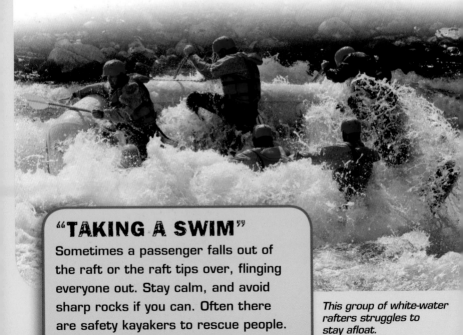

"TAKING A SWIM"

Sometimes a passenger falls out of the raft or the raft tips over, flinging everyone out. Stay calm, and avoid sharp rocks if you can. Often there are safety kayakers to rescue people.

This group of white-water rafters struggles to stay afloat.

BULL RUNNING

This bizarre Spanish tradition isn't just scary, it's completely insane. Why would you run up a street with a bunch of dangerous, charging, 1,500-pound (680 kg) bulls? But every year, people do it. It's an old ritual in the town of Pamplona, and a few other parts of Spain, too.

HOW IT BEGAN

The bull running in Pamplona takes place during the weeklong San Fermin festival every July. Part of the festival involves the sport of bullfighting, in which a bullfighter challenges a bull in a big arena called a bullring. The bulls are kept in a pen in one part of the town, and at eight o'clock in the morning, they are released to run along the streets to the bullring.

Long ago, only the keepers drove them along the street from behind. Now young men and women run with them and dodge them, showing off their courage.

WHAT ABOUT THE BULLS? Some

people think bullfighting is cruel, and would like to have it banned. But in Spain, it's an ancient cultural tradition.

IS IT DANGEROUS?

It certainly is! The bulls are very big, specially chosen for their ferocity, and have huge, sharp horns. Thirteen people have been killed while bull running since 1924, and hundreds have been badly hurt.

SCARINESS

You do not want to get near a grumpy bull.

Bull runners and the fearsome bulls tear up the dusty streets.

HUMAN CANNONBALL

Can a human being really be fired out of a cannon—basically a giant gun—like a speeding bullet? Yes—and it's been going on for well over 100 years, as a daredevil stunt or circus trick.

BANG!

With a big bang and a plume of smoke, the human cannonball shoots out of the cannon and headfirst through the air. However, the explosion and smoke are just for show. The cannon is actually powered by compressed air or a large spring—so the human cannonball doesn't get burned. If the stunt has been set up properly, they will land safely in a net or inflatable crash pad, positioned 70–120 feet (20–37 m) away.

OH NOOOOO!

It must be terrifying to realize that you're going to miss the target! Through history, plenty of performers have ended up in a crumpled heap. Others have tried to fly across a river, fallen short, and ended up hitting the water.

ZOOMING ZAZEL

The first person to perform as a human cannonball was "Zazel," a 14-year-old girl, really named Rosa Richter. She was first shot out of a spring-powered cannon in 1877.

Contemporary human cannonball Dave "Cannonball" Smith.

SCARINESS

😨 😨

Fun to watch, but it must be a bit nerve-wracking if you're the cannonball!

ZORBING

You've seen a hamster running around inside a clear plastic ball. Well, a ZORB is like a hamster ball for humans. There's a large outer sphere, and a small inner one where you sit. The space in between is filled with air, making the ball bouncy while protecting you.

NOW WHAT?

To go ZORBing (also called sphering, globe riding, or orbing) you get inside the ZORB, and roll down a hill. You and a friend or two can be strapped in place inside, or just left to tumble around freely. As the ball speeds up, you're flung against the sides and spin around and around, at up to 30 mph (50 km/h). You're quite safe, but have no control over the ZORB as it spins and swerves.

MORE ZORBING FUN

You can "ZYDRO Ride" with a few buckets of water inside the ball with you, or ZORB in complete darkness in a sphere that's not see-through. At some indoor centers, you can even sit inside a ZORB that's bouncing around on top of a giant jet of air.

Plummeting down a hill at such high speeds makes for a thrilling ride.

SCARINESS

More fun than scary, but it could make you feel sick!

ZORBING SAFETY

ZORBing accidents are rare, but have happened when ZORBs or safety nets break. Check that all the equipment is in good condition before you roll.

BIG WAVE SURFING

Surfing normal-size waves at the seaside is a lot of fun. But the bigger waves get, the scarier they are. In parts of Hawaii, California, and Australia, waves as big as 70 feet (20 m) tall can roll in. That's as high as an eight-story building. And some people surf them!

HOW DO THEY DO IT?

Surfers normally paddle on their boards past where the waves break, and catch a rolling wave as it comes along. But to surf bigger waves, you have to go faster. You can use an extra large, fast surfboard designed for big wave surfing. Or a Jet Ski can tow you into the right place. This method, called tow-in surfing, lets surfers use smaller boards that are easier to control, so they can ride the biggest waves of all.

WAVES OF FEAR

The weight and force of a giant wave are incredibly powerful. It could smash boats to splinters. While a surfer stays on the surface and clear of the breaking wave they're safe. But if they have a wipeout, in which they fall in and go under the wave as it breaks, the wave will push them deep underwater. They have to struggle back to the surface before the next wave comes. If they don't make it, they can get thrown against rocks.

SCARINESS

Some of the giant waves that surf ride are truly terrifying!

SHARK SNACK

Surfers are among those at risk of a shark attack (see page 10). Besides being in the water a lot, they can look a bit like seals or sea lions from below as they paddle their boards.

ZIP LINING

Maybe you've tried a mini-zip line in an adventure playground. It has a handle or a rubber seat dangling from a wire, and you climb on and zoom along, just above the ground. A real zip line is a bit like this, but longer and much, much higher.

WHAT'S IT FOR?

Zip lines are set up for tourists in places like forests and national parks, so that they can whizz through, getting a great view of the wildlife. Sometimes climbers or filmmakers use them to reach remote spots such as the top of a sea stack (a rock standing in the sea).

WHEEEEE!

Most simple zip lines work by gravity. A typical zip line starts somewhere high, and a series of zip lines takes you down to ground level. On a really long, steep line, you can build up amazing speeds of up to 65 mph (100 km/h). Some zip lines carry you high over cliffs, gorges, or rivers. In Hawaii, you can even zip off the top of a volcano—seriously scary!

Tourists enjoy the sunny view in downtown Vancouver, Canada.

SCARINESS

could be a breeze, or scare you
lly—it depends how high you are!

ZIPPING TIPS Zip lines are becoming more and more common. If you'd like to try, look out for zip line adventures near you—there may be one at your nearest forest, theme park, or climbing center.

HIGH WIRE

In this traditional circus act, the performer walks along a tightly stretched rope or cable, maybe doing a few tricks, too, like dangling from the wire. Some superbrave wire walkers have also performed nail-biting challenges, such as walking across gorges or waterfalls.

SCARINESS

When you see how far there is to fall, you wonder why they do it!

HOW DO THEY DO IT?

Balancing on a narrow wire is very tricky. You need years of practice to be good at it. Walkers also wear special soft shoes that help them feel and grip the wire. You have to be calm and cool—you can't start to panic halfway across!

SPINE-TINGLING STUNTS

In the 1850s, French stuntman Jean-François Gravelet became famous for his high-wire feats over Niagara Falls, on the border between the United States and Canada. He crossed the falls in daring ways: carrying another man on his back, by bicycle, and on stilts. Once, he even took a stove, and cooked an omelet on the high wire! Philippe Petit walked a wire between the Twin Towers of the former World Trade Center.

BALANCING ACT

Walking the high wire carrying a long pole is actually easier. As long as the pole is bendy, it hangs down a little on either side of the walker, helping them to stay balanced.

Philippe Petit on a treacherous high wire in Paris, France.

TRAPEZE

A trapeze is pretty simple—it's basically a stick dangling from two ropes. But a skilled circus trapeze troupe can make you gasp and cover your eyes in terror as they swoop through the air, leaping from one swinging trapeze to another, or somersaulting across to a teammate waiting to catch their hands or feet.

TRAPEZE TRICKS

Aerialists (trapeze performers) make it look easy, but in fact dangling from a trapeze is hard work. Experienced aerialists practice hard until they can do incredible tricks like somersaulting three times in the air before being caught, or hanging from the trapeze by one leg.

STATIC TRAPEZE

A trapeze you swing on is known as a flying trapeze, but you can also perform on a single trapeze hanging straight down—a static (or still) trapeze. Sound a bit boring? Not when it's hanging from a helicopter or over a cliff! Daredevil aerialists have done stunts on static trapezes hundreds of feet in the air.

GIVE IT A GO!

You might want to try the trapeze in an exercise class. It's quite safe, since you are secured with a rope and there's a safety net.

Trapeze lessons at Whistler ski resort, Canada.

SCARINESS

Relying on someone to catch your ankles must be daunting.

MOTORBIKE JUMPING

The rider kick-starts the engine and roars into action, zooming fast in a dead straight line. Ahead of him is a giant ramp. The bike shoots up the ramp and sails into the air. Will he land safely, or fall short?

A crazy stunt performed in midair.

MAKING THE JUMP

Doing a motorbike jump takes guts, skill, and experience—and a reliable bike. It can only work if the rider takes off correctly from the first ramp, and lands smoothly on the second. They must also keep the bike balanced while in the air, and, of course, they can't lose their nerve. Once you're committed to the jump, you have to go for it.

WHITE-KNUCKLE RIDES

In 2010 Australian rider Robbie "Maddo" Maddison leaped 280 feet (85 m) over the Corinth Canal in Greece—which runs between two cliffs. In the middle, the bike was 311 feet (95 m) above the water. Maddison also did a backflip jump across London's Tower Bridge.

SCARINESS

Terrifying to watch—but most big jumpers do know what they're doing.

CRASH! A jump can go wrong if you're not going fast enough to clear the gap, or if you lose control of the bike in the air. Stunt riders wear helmets and loads of padded gear, but a crash can be disastrous.

SWORD SWALLOWING

Sword swallowing looks as if it might be an illusion—maybe using trick swords that fold up, or somehow hiding them instead of actually swallowing them. But no—sword swallowers really do put a sword, or sometimes several, right down their throats. How do they do it?

SCARINESS

As long as you leave it to the professionals, it's not too scary.

Don't try this at home.

OPEN WIDE

When a sword is swallowed, it goes into the mouth, past the throat, and down the esophagus, the tube leading to the stomach—and sometimes right into the stomach, too! Normally, this is a tight, bendy route. To open it up and straighten it out, the sword swallower has to tip their head back and relax their swallowing muscles.

SWALLOW YOUR FEAR

Sword swallowing is NOT good for you. It gives you a sore throat, and can cut a hole in your esophagus—ouch!

HOW MANY SWORDS? Sword swallowers keep setting new records for how many swords they can swallow at once. It can be as many as **16**, depending on how thin the swords are.

STUNT FALLING

As if the fall wasn't dangerous enough, the stuntperson may have to fall after being "shot" or smashing through a window, or even fall while set on fire!

ARE THEY REALLY FALLING?

Not always! For some stunt falls, the stuntman or woman wears a harness fixed to a thin, strong wire. They are then lowered down very quickly by rope. Or they can fall attached to a type of bungee cord, measured to make them almost hit the ground. The film is then edited to take out the cord or cable, and make the fall look real.

A flaming stuntperson falls onto an air bag that's waiting below.

FREE FALL

Falling properly through the air, from heights of up to 200 feet (60 m), really takes guts. To do this, stuntpeople have to jump accurately onto a landing pack or air bag, positioning themselves to land safely on their back. The landing area can be made of prepared piles of cardboard boxes that collapse on impact, or it can be a big, specially designed bag full of air.

SCARINESS

If a stunt is done well, it should l[ook] real and be scary to watch!

NO BOUNCING!

If you're imagining an inflatable crash pad, a bit like a balloon, think again! A stunt landing pack has openings that let air out slowly.

STORM CHASING

Storm chasing is exactly what it sounds like—chasing after storms to get a really good view of them. Usually, storm chasers track down big thunderstorms and, if possible, tornadoes—incredibly powerful, spiraling, funnel-shaped windstorms. They're breathtaking to watch, but also seriously scary if you get too close.

WHY CHASE STORMS?

There are actually lots of different reasons to go storm chasing, and lots of different people who do it. Meteorologists (weather scientists) like to get close to storms to see how they work. News journalists chase storms to report on them. There are also hobby storm chasers.

SCARY STORM SIGHTINGS

To find good storms, storm chasers track weather patterns and forecasts, and drive to where storm activity is expected. They look out for the telltale signs of a tornado, such as a roaring sound and a greenish-looking sky. A tornado can "hop" (suddenly shift position). They have to be careful!

DID YOU KNOW?

The risk of being sucked up by a tornado makes storm chasing feel scary. But the riskiest thing about it is actually people driving too fast, or not paying attention.

SCARINESS

If they're lucky, storm chasers get a close-up view of a tornado!

Storm chasers in Kansas drive dangerously close to a supercell thunderstorm—a storm capable of producing a tornado.

ACKNOWLEDGMENTS

Marshall Editions would like to thank the following for their kind permission to reproduce their images.

Key: t = top   b = bottom   c = center   r = right   l = left   bgr = background

Cover, clockwise from top left: UPI Photo/Carlos Gutierrez; Shutterstock/Brett Mulcahy; Shutterstock/EVRON; Shutterstock/Edwin Verin; Shutterstock/Ivan Cholakov Gostock-dot-net; Shutterstock/Audrey Snider-Bell.

Pages: 1 Shutterstock/Chudakov; 2–3 Corbis/LA Daily News/Gene Blevins; 4–5 Alamy/Art Directors & TRIP; 6–7 Shutterstock/Christope Michot; 8 Science Photo Library/NOAA; 9 Nature Picture Library/Martin Dohrn; 10 Nature Picture Library/Jeff Rotman; 11 Ardea/Thomas Marent; 12 Ardea/John Daniels; 13 Nature Picture Library/Daniel Heuclin; 14 Photo Library/Tim Scoones; 15 Corbis/Roger Ressmeyer; 16 Alamy/Westend61 GmbH; 17 Alamy/Peter Arnold, Inc.;18t Corbis/Paul Souders; 18b Corbis; 19 The Kobal Collection/Warner Bros; 20 Reuters/Stringer Australia; 21 Corbis/Galen Rowell; 22 Alamy/Graham Hughes; 23 Corbis/Andrew Brownbill; 24 Corbis/Arctic-Images; 25 Corbis/Mike Hollingshead; 26 Shutterstock/Melanie Metz; 27 Shutterstock/Sybille Yates; 28 Alamy/Theirry Grun; 29 Public Domain/Tuohirulla; 30 Alamy/Mike Goldwater; 31 Getty/Oliver Furrer; 32 Shutterstock/Molodec; 33 Science Photo Library/Daniel L. Osborne; 34t Science Photo Library/Jim Reed; 34c Science Photo Library/Jim Edds; 35 Alamy/Andrew McConnell; 36 Shutterstock/StijntS; 37 Photolibrary/Cahir Davitt; 38 Alamy/MARKA; 39 Getty/Keren Su; 40 Shutterstock/Ttphoto; 41 Alamy/Damon Coulter; 42 Corbis/Keystone/Arno Balzarini; 43 Corbis/Jonathan Blair; 44 Jeffrey Kwan; 45bgr Alamy/Paul Thompson; 45c Corbis/Imaginechina; 46bgr and 46c Corbis/National Geographic Society/John Burcham; 47bgr Alamy/Collpicto; 47b Corbis/Paul A. Souders; 48 Shutterstock/Natalia Bratslavsky; 49 Corbis/Eddi Boehnke; 50 Alamy/Tim Whitby; 51 Alamy/Edward North; 52 Alamy/Steve Hamblin; 53 Topfoto; 54 Corbis/Patrick Ward; 55 Alamy/The Marsden Archive; 56 Alamy/The Marsden Archive; 57 Corbis/Jean-Pierre Lescourret; 58 Corbis/Jonathan Blail; 59 Alamy/Gary Doak; 60 Shutterstock/Janos Levente; 61 Shutterstock/Margaret M Stewart; 62 Corbis/Antonino Barbagallo; 63 Shutterstock/Russell Swain; 64 Alamy/Christian Darkin; 65 Alamy/Dale O'Dell; 66 Alamy/Jan Tadeusz; 67 Alamy/Steve Bielschowsky; 68 Shutterstock/loriklaszlo; 69 Science Photo Library/Victor Habbick Visions; 70 Fortean Picture Library/Ella Louise Fortune; 71 Shutterstock/Markus Gann; 72 Getty/Thinkstock; 73 Alamy/Gaertner; 74 Science Picture Library/J.G. Golden; 75 Alamy/Robert Harding Picture Library Ltd; 76 Science Photo Library/NASA; 77 NASA/CXC/M. Weiss; 78 Science Photo Library/3D4Medical.com; 79 Science Photo Library/Eye of Science; 80 Science Photo Library/Tim Vernon; 81 Corbis/Thomas Roepke; 82 Alamy/Peter M. Wilson; 83 Shutterstock/Terrance Emerson; 84 Alamy/Rex; 85 Reuters/Marko Djurica; 86 Getty/Ken Fisher; 87 Getty/Oliver Furrer; 88 Shutterstock/Vitalii Nesterchuk; 89 Getty/William R Sallaz; 90 Alamy/RIA Novosti; 91 Alamy/Travelscape Images; 92 Corbis/Dusko Despotovic; 93 Alamy/blickwinkel; 94 Getty/Stephen Alvarez; 95 Alamy/Jeremy Sutton-Hibbert; 96 Corbis/Rolf Kosecki; 97 Corbis/Mike Powell; 98 Corbis/Aurora Photos/Keith Ladzinski; 99 Corbis/Thilo Brunner; 100 Corbis/David Madison; 101 Corbis/EPA/Jim Hollander; 102 Alamy/Agripicture Images; 103 Shutterstock/Chris Turner; 104 Getty/Rick Hyman; 105 Corbis/EPA/Kim Ludbrook; 106 Corbis/Sygma/Patrick Durand; 107 Alamy/WorldFoto; 108 Alamy/Chris McLennan; 109 Shutterstock/Antonio Petrone; 110 Alamy/celebrity; 111 Corbis/Jim Reed